RECLAIM YOUR NEST EGG

RECLAIM YOUR NEST EGG

Take Control of Your Financial Future

KEN KAMEN

with DALE BURG

BLOOMBERG PRESS
An Imprint of
WILEY

Published by John Wiley & Sons, Inc., Hoboken, New Jersey.
Published simultaneously in Canada.

For general information on our other products and services or for technical support, please
contact our Customer Care Department within the United States at (800) 762-2974, outside
the United States at (317) 572-3993 or fax (317) 572-4002.

Wiley also publishes its books in a variety of electronic formats. Some content that appears in
print may not be available in electronic books. For more information about Wiley products,
visit our web site at www.wiley.com.

Library of Congress Cataloging-in-Publication Data:

Kamen, Ken.
  Reclaim your nest egg : take control of your financial future / Ken Kamen with Dale Burg.
    p. cm.—(Bloomberg ; 47)
  Includes index.
  ISBN 978-1-57660-370-3 (hardback)
    1. Retirement income—Planning.   2. Finance, Personal.   3. Investments.   I. Burg,
Dale. II. Title.
  HG179.K357   2010
  332.024—dc22
                                                                    2010021346

Printed in the United States of America

10 9 8 7 6 5 4 3 2 1

I dedicate this book to my parents, Johanna and Irwin Kamen.

The lessons I learned from them have served as the foundation for whatever successes I have had since leaving their nest. Were it not for their diligence and judgment in building up their own next egg, my life would have taken a completely different path. I would not have had the courage to ride out the less-than-stellar financial period I experienced shortly after starting a brokerage firm in 1988. It was immensely reassuring to know that if everything crashed around me, my parents would be there, willing and able to keep my family afloat without jeopardizing their own financial future. Thankfully, I was able to get through that tough time without having to ask for help. From my point of view, the best return my parents' nest egg ever produced never showed up on their balance sheet.

And I also dedicate this book to my daughters and my wife.

Samantha and Emily are my inspiration and the compass that guides all that I do. An interviewer once asked my life's goals. They're simple: to make my daughters proud of me every day. They have taught me what is truly important in life.

I can never repay my wife Andrea for her patience, guidance, and encouragement—throughout our lifetime together and especially while I was working on this book. She never complained about being a "book widow"—left alone on nights and weekends as I discovered how difficult it is to be an author. I love her with all of my heart and I am grateful every day that she chose to spend her life with me.

Contents

Prologue   1

1   Reconsider the Future   5

2   Rightsize Your Plans   21

3   Dump the Head Trash   41

4   Ignore the Noise   59

5   Check the Fine Print   79

6   Embrace a Game Plan   95

7   Establish Your Rules   115

8   Reconstruct Your Portfolio   135

9   Employ Defensive Moves   163

10   Take the Helm   183

Epilogue   195

Acknowledgments   203

About the Author   205

Index   207

RECLAIM YOUR NEST EGG

Prologue

HOW CAN YOU reclaim something you never fully possessed?

The whipsawing of the markets for the past couple of decades has taken away everyone's confidence. We've gone three steps forward and two steps back and lurched between euphoria and depression so often that many investors are queasy and discouraged.

"I did what I was supposed to do. I looked at the long term," they say. "But I'm still living with uncertainty. I don't want to wait until the end of each day to know whether I'm going to be able to sleep at night."

An egg is strong but not invulnerable. It needs protection from predators and the forces of nature. Your nest egg needs protection as well. Reclaiming it means taking full responsibility for it. Chances are that until now, that might not have been the case.

Instead, you gave up control. You gave it up to the "head trash"— your emotions—so you made irrational and impulsive decisions. You gave it up to the Internet and the 24-hour-a-day news channels—the very innovations that were supposed to make it easier to incubate your nest egg but instead prompted you to act rashly or paralyzed you with information overload. You gave it up to salespeople who were under pressure to pressure you into buying financial products that neither of you understood. And you gave it up to procrastination and neglect, managing your money on an ad hoc basis instead of coming up with a strategy, core principles, and a holistic approach.

You have to stop reacting and start acting. This book will help you see how you gave up control in the past and show you how to get it back.

There are lots of books that provide you with strategies for success. This book is about finding your *own* strategy—one that suits your budget, your temperament, your lifestyle, and your goals.

1

The generation now contemplating retirement took its first collective gulp in October 1987. In a five-day period, the major indexes of market valuation in the United States dropped 30 percent or more. There have been many roller coaster rides since then. Cumulatively, they've underscored your need to know the basics of the factors that affect your finances and how they all fit together.

Instead of spending time bemoaning your missteps, take advantage of how these experiences stress-tested your plan and exposed its cracks. Use the lessons you've been taught as an opportunity to put your nest egg back together and to insulate it from risk more effectively in the future.

You do not need to become an expert in all things financial. But just as you can't completely outsource the responsibility for your family's physical health, you can't do it for your family's financial health. Anyway, blaming "the system" for the loss of your financial security and peace of mind does nothing to help you reclaim them.

Where do you begin? How do you calculate a budget for your lifestyle, rightsize your expectations, and control your emotions? What should you be doing to protect yourself? How can you make a financial plan that is sound enough to last the rest of your life?

I firmly believe that you are the best person to prepare yourself for whatever lies ahead. And after 30 years of counseling investors, I have a pretty good idea of how to help you do that. As the founder of two brokerage firms and a registered investment advisor, I have talked to thousands of clients. I have employed over 200 financial profession-als and had the final responsibility of overseeing tens of thousands of their clients' portfolios. As a result, I've had an unusual opportunity to get an up-close and intimate look at how people deal with their money, and I have been struck by two observations in particular.

One is that whereas everyone has the same long-term goal—to prepare for a comfortable and secure future—no two people view their personal finances exactly the same way. The pattern of our decisions seems as distinctive as our fingerprints.

The second is that the overwhelming majority of people are very committed to the *idea* of building for the future but they have no real interest in the specifics of how that should be accomplished. They are easily satisfied with superficial explanations for making deeply consequential financial decisions. That explains the astonishing fact that the brokers and advisors with the most clients are often the best salesmen rather than the most qualified financial professionals.

I know firsthand how much work and attention to detail it takes to amass assets, so I'll never understand why so many people are willing to abandon their habits of diligence and care when it comes to overseeing the fruit of their life's work. Once you've built up your retirement fund, you become a wealth manager. Ready or not, you have to devise and follow a strategy to make your assets last the rest of your life.

But here's the big unknown: How long will "the rest of your life" be? A report on retirement from the Society of Actuaries in 2006 indicated that significant numbers of people close to retirement seriously underestimated longevity risk—that is, the risk of outliving your money. One out of every two people who are now 65 is likely to celebrate a 90th birthday. Yet most of them haven't planned for that eventuality.

There are plenty of books about saving for retirement, and quite a few that deal with the issues of finding the right retirement lifestyle. There are a handful that give very particular advice for dealing with a pension or your 401(k) allocations, for decumulation and avoiding taxes on your retirement funds.

But before you deal with the particulars, you need a macro view of the issues affecting your financials:

- Making a realistic assessment of the lifestyle your resources can provide while getting you to a finish line that may be decades away.

- Not falling prey to psychological pitfalls that can be especially devastating to irreplaceable retirement funds.

- Not allowing the noise from the media to divert and derail you from your long-term perspective.

- Learning how to exercise the same caution and skepticism when buying financial products as you do when making other purchases.

- Creating a game plan that's so comprehensive and well-designed—and so right for you—that it merits your absolute commitment.

- Establishing investment principles that serve as your personal Commandments.

- Coming up with a process that provides holistic, dynamic oversight to ensure that your plan is continually appropriate.

Most people I see aren't thinking about a process. Like the folks who show up at the accountant with a shoebox full of canceled checks, receipts, and other bits and pieces, they come in to me with a virtual shoebox containing their financial life. Inside is a disparate collection of financial "stuff" they have amassed over a lifetime with no clear understanding of how it all happened. Even before recent events, most plans were already in pieces that didn't fit together.

It's time to re-engineer: to create a structurally sound plan that will withstand turbulence, get you to the finish line, and even allow you to leave a legacy.

After any Wall Street decline, the greatest danger is not that the markets won't come back. They will. It's that once people lose trust and confidence, they position their assets in a way that is unlikely to cover their needs for a lifetime. Fearing danger everywhere, they move to the sidelines and put their money into the proverbial mattress—resulting in low yield, little growth, and little inflation protection. Feeling let down by the industry, they are wary of professional advice and reluctant to rely on anyone.

Reclaiming what's yours is a matter of making a realistic assessment of your own situation and going back to the basics. You have to understand how things got away from you in the first place. You have to do your homework, and determine what resources you need to keep your nest egg safe.

The broader and deeper your knowledge of all that is involved in planning your financial future, the more you will want to know. There isn't a book on the shelves—including this one—that can give you a plan for your specific situation. However, the more questions this book inspires you to ask, the more progress you'll make in reaching your goal, and I'll have accomplished mine.

Reconsider
the Future

IF WE WERE BORN with expiration dates on our rear ends, retirement planning would be a piece of cake. But that's not how it goes.

Calculating how many years to plan for is one challenge. Another is that you need to grow your money to achieve your goals. In doing so, you will be exposing the fruits of your life's labor to significant volatility. Your capital will be bouncing around when markets go from euphoria to despair.

Such fluctuations are beyond your control. After the market began its free fall in mid-2008, people contemplating retirement and retirees, like all investors, were reminded once again of just how vulnerable we all are. When the accumulated assets of a lifetime go into a steep decline just as your earning years are coming to an end, it can be especially painful.

Stunned investors, seeing massive amounts of their money vaporize, second-guessed their past portfolio decisions and started to recognize that not having less is just as important as striving for more.

Lessons from the Past

It's important to bear in mind that our financial system has withstood many past shocks. Before the recent debacle, we had the Great Depression and, several decades later, the malaise of the 1970s.

In the 1980s, the failure of over 1,000 banks in the savings and loan disaster cost taxpayers about $124 billion and the market dipped 30.6 percent in one five-day period in October 1987. In the next decade and a half, the market rebounded and enjoyed its best period ever.

Then came the dot-com bubble, which began in 1995, peaked in March 2000—when the NASDAQ hit 5,100—and burst in 2001. The blame for this one could be pinned on the investing public, which stopped looking at traditional means to evaluate stocks and just went on an irrational buying spree, as if somehow new technologies had changed all the rules.

More recently, we witnessed a series of corporate scandals. It started with Enron, which filed for bankruptcy in 2001, and also involved Adelphia, Global Crossing, WorldCom, and others. The causes were questionable and even fraudulent accounting, and in an attempt to halt such practices, Congress passed the Sarbanes-Oxley Act of 2002.

Despite these problems, and even after the shock waves created by the terrorist attacks of 9/11, the market has always recovered and, in fact, gone on to climb higher.

I've always liked the adage that defines bear markets as periods when the people who think this time is different sell all their holdings to the people who know this time is never different.

Sharing the Blame

The events of 2008 were precipitated by a bubble in housing prices, the blame for which can surely be spread around. Banks and financial institutions made ill-advised mortgages readily available, homebuyers snapped them up recklessly, and investors backed the whole practice without fully investigating what they were buying.

Like past declines, the latest one wasn't caused by a breakdown in the economic system but because everyone lost sight of the fact that fundamentals really do matter. No matter how thinly you slice it or how globally you distribute it, a bad investment is still a bad investment.

The framework for the latest debacle was laid when, bowing to the requests of banking industry lobbyists, the government relaxed many long-standing regulations and safeguards. The banks were allowed to make riskier investments and permitted to monitor themselves.

The government-sponsored, shareholder-owned companies that buy mortgages from banks and lenders began making investments in less conservative mortgages, relying on computer models that didn't anticipate large numbers of mortgage holders defaulting at once. Inflated executive compensation, based on short-term profits rather than long-term consequences, also contributed to the meltdown.

Business moves in cycles, so an eventual downturn was to be expected. Though recent events were caused in large part by corporate ignorance, greed, and malfeasance, it's also important to recognize the culpability of the public. Adam Smith, the famous economist, championed the idea that allowing people to act in their own-self interest—that is, allowing free markets and taking a laissez-faire attitude—would result in prosperity for everyone.

Yet when the market started to crash and burn in the fall of 2008, in testimony before a Congressional House Oversight Committee, Federal Reserve Chairman Alan Greenspan said, "Those of us who have looked to the self-interest of lending institutions to protect shareholders' equity are in a state of shocked disbelief." While Smith's view of self-interest assumed a high level of morality and rational behavior, that assumption proved unfounded.

There is more than enough blame to go around: borrowers making bets on home values going up; politicians making it easier for everyone to buy homes; brokers lending money to underqualified buyers; bankers selling packages of risky debt; and investors seeking opportunities without knowing what they were buying and without heed to protecting their financial futures.

The world engaged in a massive game of kick the can. While everyone may have understood that risk was real, they believed they could just pass it along to the next guy. Then everything collapsed and everyone was reminded that there are no free lunches.

Unfortunately, making one of the most common investment mistakes—chasing performance—exaggerated the pain for many people. During the real estate bubble, financial stocks were soaring because of the phantom income they were creating, and many investors were heavily weighted in this sector.

You know how the fine print always says, "Past performance is no guarantee of future performance"? Most people don't heed that warning, but the fact is that investing based only on performance as a guide is investing in the past, not the future.

The damage done to retirement plans and portfolios was a wakeup call. Many people, even very smart people, had checked their brains at the door, designating others to think for them and trusting that somehow the "system" would safeguard their assets.

Redefining Retirement

Even before the events of the recent past, people who are currently in the process of planning for retirement faced some unique challenges. To know why, step back a little and think how deeply the expectation of retirement is built into the popular consciousness. It's easy to lose sight of the fact that it's a relatively new concept without much precedent. The idea that the majority of Americans would be able to put their working days behind them and look forward to comfortable, enjoyable years of leisure has been a reality for only a single generation.

A century ago, only the members of the upper classes enjoyed good enough health and sufficient funds to ensure a pleasurable old age. Most U.S. workers were either farmers or artisans. If they were lucky, they kept on working until they dropped in their tracks. If, however, they were impaired by some disease or accident, they had to rely on the goodwill of family members to take care of them until the end came.

Some people credit German chancellor Otto von Bismarck with "inventing" retirement. In the late 1880s, he put into effect a government plan to help people 65 and older. Since, in those days, the average lifespan was only about 45 years, the program was more like disability insurance than a retirement plan.

Still others believe that retirement was a byproduct of mass production. Factory owners gave a severance package to ease out the aging workers who couldn't keep up the pace on the assembly line. When that happened, like the factory jobs that helped create it, the idea of retirement became standardized.

Social *In*security

Then, in 1934, retirement became institutionalized: Social Security, which started as something called Old People's Relief, was established. Like the severance packages that had been created about 50 years earlier, it was meant to ease out older workers, but during the Depression, the primary goal was to free up jobs for young male heads of households.

Social Security had the effect of establishing retirement as happening at a set point in time—at age 65. It also established the concept of retirement as a general entitlement, since it protected people who had no prospects for an income in the years when they could no longer work. But since the average lifespan in 1934 was only 61 years, the establishment of Social Security wasn't initially transformative.

However, within a decade, World War II was coming to a close. In the booming postwar economy, businesses could afford to offer perks in order to attract young and capable employees. Those perks included long-term job security for workers and, at the end of their tenures, generous pensions.

With the prospect of Social Security plus a pension, supplemented with whatever savings they could put aside, a new generation—that is, the parents of baby boomers—could truly look forward to retirement.

But even as the first wave of people who paid into the program are still getting their benefits, the Social Security program faces an uncertain future. The population of the United States is aging. It is likely there will soon be fewer workers paying into the system than there are people of retirement age.

There are various fixes available to shore up the system—for example, increase the percentages of contributions, reduce benefits, deny payments to people whose income is over a certain level, institute some combination of the above—but, not surprisingly, none of these has attracted popular support.

As a result, the Social Security Board of Trustees in 2006 estimated that payroll tax revenue would fall below the cost of benefits in 2017, that the Medicare fund will be depleted in 2018, and that the Social Security trust fund will be exhausted in 2040.

On March 25, 2010, the *New York Times* noted in a front-page story ("Social Security to See Payout Exceed Pay-In This Year") that "This year, the system will pay out more in benefits than it receives in payroll taxes, an important threshold it was not expected to cross until at least 2016, according to the Congressional Budget Office."

More Holes in Your Safety Net

But even if Social Security were to remain in place, it's a pretty flimsy net. Whereas lower-income workers with a long work history may find that it replaces a large share of their income, the more robust your lifestyle has been, the less meaningful a factor it will be for putting together a long-term retirement plan. And for most Americans, the standard of living has grown exponentially in the postwar years.

Another former source of retirement income, pension money, is also no longer much of a factor in protecting your future. Some companies still offer traditional pensions, but most have dropped them. They're expensive to fund, and compliance is time-consuming. And although, at one time, they were an effective recruitment device, that is no longer the case. Today's workers can't imagine a lifetime spent at one company and are accustomed to portable plans. So instead of attracting young and desirable new employees, pensions simply encourage older workers to hang around until they can retire.

Although your parents' generation relied on the management work of a government agency and a company's pension department to fund their retirement, pensions and Social Security for new retirees have been replaced by what I call *individual insecurity*. In fact, Americans are learning they cannot abandon personal responsibility, whether it is to the government, to corporations, or to the financial services industry.

It's Up to You

"Thirty years ago, a typical consumer had a fixed-rate mortgage, a life-insurance policy, a bank account and an employer-paid pension plan," wrote Eleanor Laise in the *Wall Street Journal* on November 25, 2008 ("Some Consumers Say Wall Street Failed Them"). She continued: "Nowadays, that same consumer may have a payment option adjustable-rate mortgage, a 401(k) retirement-savings plan, a home-equity line of credit and perhaps even a health-savings account, instead of traditional employer-sponsored health insurance.

"In the process, risks previously borne by big banks and employers have been placed squarely on the shoulders of consumers. Individuals increasingly bear the risk of interest-rate fluctuations, rising health-care costs, stock-market gyrations and [the italics are mine here] *outliving their retirement savings.*"

Personal financial management always involves some risk, but retirement planning presents unique challenges. You have less time to ride out the cycles, and unanticipated responsibility for others may be a larger factor in your considerations.

What's more, your focus in retirement is on *decumulation* rather than accumulation—thinking about strategies for spending rather than for acquisition. Still, what ultimately determines how successful your plan will be is none of the foregoing. It's all about how effectively you anticipate and manage risk.

Whereas inflation risk (the prospect of rising prices) and investment risk (the possibility that you'll put money where it doesn't perform well) represent potential problems, the single biggest issue you have to face is *longevity risk*: the chance of having your assets flat-line before you do. You run a far greater risk of outliving your money than of squandering it.

That's largely because preventive medicine and new drugs, therapies, and surgical procedures have dramatically extended life expectancy. The Census Bureau projects that boy babies born in the United States in 2010 can expect to live 75.6 years, and girl babies, 80.8 years. But those numbers don't take into account the fact that the older you are already, the more likely it is you'll live longer than average.

Life *Isn't* Short

We all know how hard it is to deal with the idea of your own mortality. But it appears that conceiving of your own potential longevity is equally difficult. According to a 2006 report from the Society of Actuaries, although people are aware that life expectancy is increasing, at least six out of ten people underestimate their own.

In other words, although they understand the idea of aggregate longevity risk (which is the possibility that a group of their contemporaries will live to a very old age), they somehow can't reconcile that with the idea of select longevity risk (which is the possibility that they themselves will do so). In fact, as the former becomes increasingly likely, so does the latter. That is, the more very old people there are, the greater the chance that *you yourself* will live to be a very old person.

Hallmark now expects to sell 85,000 "Happy 100th Birthday" cards annually, and people who live to be 100 or older are the fastest-growing segment of the population. Perhaps the White House will stop sending out birthday cards to centenarians by the year 2050. If the demographers are right that there will be a million 100-year-olds in this country at that time, the gesture might be too costly.

"Far too many retirees grossly underappreciate the implications of longevity for their financial needs," the Society of Actuaries report says, "especially if they should turn out to be among those surviving into their 10th decade." Statistics suggest that if you make it to age 65, you have a pretty good shot at living 25 more years, an opportunity that should not be clouded by the concern that you will run out of money.

Of course, feeling stressed about the future is itself one solution: It can take years off your life. But I think most people would prefer to have a plan. The way to start is by getting a picture of the personal universe you envision. Whatever you haven't taken into consideration can set your plan off course.

Don't Count on a Paycheck

I can't tell you how often I hear people say that they don't need a retirement plan because they don't intend to retire. They'll just keep on working. Some people might consider that optimistic, but as a financial advisor, I'd call it delusional.

Hoping to work is one thing. *Expecting* to work is another. You can't base a future on the assumption you'll remain physically and mentally employable. Nor can you presume that there will always be people interested in hiring you.

You frequently hear the estimate that 80 percent of jobs are gotten through someone you know. As you get older, your job-prospecting network gets smaller. Fewer of your contemporaries are likely to be working themselves, so they're less likely to be able to hire you, recommend you, or even hear about job opportunities to pass along. Younger people who are in charge of hiring are more likely to bring in a peer or a younger person than someone their parents' age.

Business practices change, too. Software is upgraded and systems get revamped. Employers don't see much incentive in training an older person who has a limited number of years left in the work force.

But I'm sure you have lots of anecdotal evidence that the picture is not totally bleak. There are plenty of older people who remain in the work force, and there are ways that you can handle your career as an asset class and raise the possibility that you'll be hired. But you have to consider the possibility that you can't and you won't.

You Can't Predict Health Costs

Another risk factor is becoming incapacitated. That's another topic you hear a lot about. People say things like, "If I start losing it, just shoot me." Or, "I'm going to stockpile pills." I suppose everyone has a mental vision of being unable to function, and in their heads, they picture themselves struck down by a spectacular crisis that leaves them completely helpless.

But the reality is that you're far more likely to be blindsided by a more mundane and less dramatic problem, such as back pain that makes it impossible for you to sit at a desk all day or arthritis that prevents you from getting behind the wheel of a car. Even a reversible problem might put you in rehabilitation temporarily or require some type of paid assistance. And a problem doesn't have to be catastrophic to be long term—or costly.

It seems probable that health costs will continue their upward spiral, and what will happen with Medicare is problematic. In any event, the program is under pressure because of the increasing numbers of people aging into the system and the fact that their numbers are disproportionate to the workers paying into the system. Together with the ongoing deficit in the federal budget, that just adds an extra layer of uncertainty regarding the support Medicare will be able to offer over the long term.

Even now, there are gaps in coverage. Recently I was talking to a woman who needs a very sophisticated hearing aid that must be connected to a battery inserted behind her ear in an outpatient procedure. That hearing aid, together with a more conventional one for her other ear, might cost $10,000, and both devices are expected to last only five years. The surgeon's and anesthesiologist's fees, plus hospital costs, might run as high as $30,000. Still, because she's over 65, I had assumed that at least Medicare and her supplemental insurance would cover some of the cost, but she said that's not the case.

Although her audiologist tried to get the insurers to change their position, they could not be budged. Their representatives explained to the audiologist that the companies would allocate money to procedures and equipment that prolonged life; but they would not necessarily reimburse expenses that simply improved the *quality* of life. Her situation is a good example of how the burden of unexpected medical costs can put your retirement planning into jeopardy.

Those who have employer-provided health insurance that covers them into retirement have some hedge against spiraling costs, but they're in the minority. The Center for Retirement Research, in March 2010, reported that lifetime uninsured health care costs for a typical married couple age 65 are $197,000, including insurance premiums, out-of-pocket costs, and home heath costs, but can go as high as $311,000; and when nursing home costs are included, they have a 5 percent risk of exceeding $570,000.*

Who's Counting on You?

Another type of risk to factor into your planning is the result of a new phenomenon: being part of the so-called "sandwich" generation. As I point out to my clients, generally we model our behavior after the people who preceded us. Observing how Dad got burned in the stock market or how Uncle Pete made a bundle in real estate helps us avoid mistakes and formulate our own plans.

But it's unlikely your retirement will be like Uncle Pete's or your dad's. When they were in their 50s and planning retirement, they weren't figuring on being asset managers in their 80s. So you can't use their behavior as a template. What's more, chances are that they, too, are living longer than they had planned for and may even be looking to *you* for support. In fact:

■ A century ago, fewer than 7 percent of people in their 60s had at least one parent still alive, says financial gerontologist Neal Cutler, who studies the effect of aging on finances. Now, almost half of all 50-year-olds do.

■ In 1989, only 60 percent of people ages 41 to 59 had one living parent, a Gallup Survey found. According to a 2006 Pew Report, the percentage had risen to 71. And close to one-third gave the parent some financial assistance—from covering everyday needs to funding home aides or assisted-living facilities.

Your adult children may also be looking to you for assistance. The web site collegegrad.com routinely polls college graduate job seekers. Whereas 67 percent were living with their parents in 2006, the

---

* Anthony Webb and Natalia Zhivan, "What Is the Distribution of Lifetime Health Care Costs from Age 65?" crr.bc.edu/researchers/anthony_webb6.html.

number rose to 73 percent in 2007, 77 percent in 2008, and 80 percent in 2009. The trend doesn't seem likely to reverse: The rise wasn't due only to the economy, the report said, but to the fact that living independently has become increasingly expensive, and as the population increases and the number of college graduates goes up, there's more competition for entry-level jobs.

And even landing a job isn't necessarily a guarantee of emancipation. So many young adults live alone only briefly before returning home that a phrase has been coined to describe such a turn of events: "the boomerang phenomenon."

In 2003 the Census Bureau reported that 50 percent of all 18- to 24-year-olds were living with their parents, and 27 percent of 18- to 34-year-olds were doing the same. As proof of how widespread this situation is, you have only to take note of the number of web sites dedicated specifically to the problems of living with—or supporting—adult children.

"Two-thirds (68%) [of boomers] say they are supporting an adult child financially, either as the primary (33%) or secondary (35%) source of support," said a 2006 Pew Report.

Young people are struggling to pay off college loans or having trouble finding jobs that can cover housing costs. Globalization and outsourcing have eliminated a lot of entry-level jobs, real wages have fallen, and a college degree isn't necessarily a ticket to a job upon graduation. So even in an economic recovery, young people may continue to have difficulty being completely self-supporting. But whatever the reason, a child who hasn't quite left the nest puts more pressure on your nest egg.

Even a child who has taken on adult responsibilities may still need support. The Millennials are the first generation of Americans who don't have a lock on fiscally outperforming their parents.

Your children may call on you to help finance a home for them and their families or to help underwrite the expensive advantages that you provided for them but they can't replicate for their offspring in a time when real income is on the wane—advantages like camp, private schools, and trips. Your funding might be your grandchildren's only hope to have a debt-free college education. Though you might have expected to leave money behind for your children, financing degrees for their children might be more helpful than leaving a legacy.

Here's what's certain: If you're thriving when the folks around you aren't—if you're the only one in your world with a full silo of grain—people will be knocking at your door. You may be compelled to allocate the money you earmarked for yourself to other generations with fewer resources. And the chances are that you'll live long enough to see a few of those generations, down to the great-grandchildren.

How much are you willing to forgo some of your own desires so that your parents can move to Enviable Estates instead of Adequate Acres? How long are you going to subsidize your son until he "finds himself" or fund enrichment programs for your daughter's children? Remember: There are college loans, but there aren't any loans for retirement.

How many generations can you actually help without impinging on your own independence? No matter what you eventually decide, it will be helpful to have considered all these emotional issues with deliberation rather than making an impulsive decision when you are swayed by guilt or it's too late to consider alternatives.

You Become a Wealth Manager

Any retirement plan that can stand the test of time needs to take into consideration all the risk factors you can possibly anticipate. Even if you don't continue to perform income-generating work, you still have a job. In fact, you most likely have two: part-time work as an event planner (to ensure that all that new leisure time is filled in gratifying fashion), and full-time responsibility as a wealth manager. Whether you get to enjoy the event-planning responsibilities depends a lot on how effective a wealth manager you are.

Suddenly, you're the caretaker for the pool of money you carefully built up over the course of a lifetime. You have to spend it down in accordance with a well-thought-out plan and in ways designed to meet your planned goals. Unfortunately, most people aren't comfortable with—or good at—these responsibilities.

When the Society of Actuaries asked people to rate their concerns about retirement planning, most ranked "outliving resources" as the least of their worries. Should they live five years longer than they expected, more than half thought the solution was simply to reduce expenditures. Other fallback scenarios, which they ranked from most to least likely, included dipping into money originally earmarked for heirs, depleting savings, and tapping into the value of their homes.

The Actuaries' Society report laid out the sobering likelihood that many retirees will have to fall back on those measures long before they reach average life expectancy and compound the problem by taking on debt.

In creating your retirement plan, anticipate the tremors, avoid the fault lines, and build in shock absorbers. Anticipating risk is one of the best ways to avoid catastrophe. But that's only one of several ways you can protect your future.

Key Takeaways

- **The real danger is not that you'll lose your money but that you'll outlive it.** Advances in medicine have made it increasingly likely that those of us who live to age 65 will live on to celebrate a 90th birthday. While on the one hand that's very good news, on the other it means putting aside substantial reserves. It's true that some expenses may decline as you age, but others will increase. A realistic retirement plan has to consider the demands that longevity will make on your resources.
- **Redefine your long-term goals.** If you're a beginning investor, you're probably looking for the hottest sectors and may even invest in a long shot in hopes of hitting a jackpot. Making a big score at the beginning of your income earning years can have a huge impact on your lifestyle. But the impact of a big loss at the end of your earning years will be even bigger. So as you get older, you have to shift your emphasis from getting more to *not having less*.
- **Create your own safety net.** Over the past few decades the responsibility for maintaining your standard of living in retirement has increasingly shifted to you. The greater

the success you have achieved in your earning years, the smaller the likelihood that the support system meant to fund old age—Social Security, a pension, and Medicare—will be sufficient for you. It's unlikely to maintain the lifestyle that you aspire to, and it may not even cover your needs. Since corporations and the government won't ensure your future comfort, you have to find a way to do it yourself.

■ **Others might be counting on you.** If you're in "the sandwich generation," it's not unlikely that you will be faced with the possibility of supporting grown children and aging parents in addition to covering your own financial needs. Those obligations can stress-test even the soundest financial plan. You have to make a realistic assessment of the degree to which you're able and willing to compromise your own financial security on behalf of the people you care about.

■ **Be prepared to take on the role of wealth manager.** Having spent a lifetime building up assets, in retirement you have the new responsibility of managing them. To cover your obligations and meet your goals for a period that may last for two and possibly three decades or more, you need to develop a plan that is resilient and comprehensive. Though you may be retiring from your day job, you have an ongoing responsibility to ensure that you and your family can live the life you want.

2

Rightsize
Your Plans

RETIREMENT WAS ONCE considered a time for cutting back and winding down. You'd move somewhere sunny, smell the roses, and, when it came to spending your retirement fund, you would sip from the garden hose.

But ads directed to retirees encourage you to take the kind of gulps only a fire hose can deliver. Buy a million-dollar recreational vehicle! Own a ski retreat! Buy a retirement condo at a spa! Take a round-the-world cruise!

Treating your retirement fund like a lottery jackpot is an obsolete notion. It made sense when the retirement years represented only about 10 percent of a lifetime, but not now, when it's increasingly likely you'll spend one-third of your life at leisure.

If you're lucky enough to have so many years ahead of you, that gift shouldn't be marred by concerns about how you can fund them. If you're reading this book, I imagine you're like most of my clients. They expect to be able to cover their basic needs, but they want my help to preserve their lifestyle. If they're used to going to the marina, they want to make sure they can gas up their boat. If they're used to taking three trips a year, they don't want to go down to two.

How Much Is Enough?

As you go into retirement, you're facing a period of transition—one of the most dramatic, if not *the* most dramatic, of your lifetime. You may no longer be engaged in the job that once defined you. After decades, your daily routine may change significantly. And financially, you have to make what may be the biggest transition of all, a complete 180-degree turn—changing your focus from aggressively adding to your reserves to drawing on them as cautiously as possible.

Staying where you are is a realistic hope. What's not realistic is to have a wish list that's growing when your income may not be. Almost all the advisors and books telling you how to fund your future needs have you start by calculating what you have. Often they provide worksheets. In my opinion most people have a really good off-the-top-of-the-head sense of what their assets total. What they really want to know is, "Do I have enough?"

The answer depends on how you want to live your life. That means putting yourself in the future, looking back at now.

How hard are you pressing on the gas pedal? What are your wants, and what are your needs? How much are you spending, and how much is reasonable to spend? What impact will inflation have on these plans? You have to define your vision of the future before you can come up with a solid way to fund it.

While you're working and earning money, you get a tremendous amount of satisfaction from amassing assets and saving for retirement. Knowing that there's a certain amount coming out of your paycheck regularly and being put away for the future, knowing that you're doing the right thing, is continually gratifying. It's like being on a diet or exercising regularly: You step on the scale or you check the way your slacks fit and you get your reward. With savings, the reward comes in the form of a periodic statement.

One of the biggest psychological changes in retirement is losing this kind of satisfaction. Where do you get these good feelings when you're no longer throwing another log on the pile but instead chipping away at it? Adding to the pile is comforting; taking from it creates angst.

People spend forty years or more creating a nest egg. There's plenty of advice on saving money and growing it, on building your funds for the first house, for college, and for retirement. But it's always seemed remarkable to me how little advice is available to guide you and to help you anticipate or visualize the future so that you feel empowered and secure during the phase where you harvest and live off the fruits of your labor.

A Plan for *Your* World

I don't ask, "How are things?" when I greet a friend. I ask, "How are things in *your* world," in acknowledgment of the fact that while we're all on the same planet, each of us lives in a world of his or her own. Naturally, what I think most about are the financial choices people make: where and how they want to live. I see some people who have very few indulgences and others who make all of them into necessities. I see how someone's Can't-Live-Without-It is someone else's Couldn't-Care-Less.

That's why an investor can't just go on the Web and get some generic advice. A long-term plan has to suit *your* temperament and *your* purposes. It's got to be designed just for you. Before you start thinking about investments, you have to focus on who you are; how you want to live your life; and what you want to make of your future.

And is "you" one or are "you" two? Your partner's future is aligned with yours, and you have to do your thinking together. It's been said that the happiest marriages are the ones that have lasted 35 years or more. The kids are grown and the major issues are most likely resolved. If you've been lucky enough until that point to avoid disputes over money (the number one cause of marital problems), you don't want to start then. But it takes work to arrive at a unified view of the future.

Don't postpone talking about the key issues: Where do you expect to live? What kind of a lifestyle do you envision? You'll probably need a fair amount of discussion to get your priorities clarified.

Being in a mode of maintenance and controlled depletion can cause some stress. A woman who is accustomed to indulging her shoe obsession may take offense if her husband suddenly starts to ask if she really needs to spend $250 on another pair. A man who has been used to enjoying fishing trips may become annoyed if his wife appears to begrudge the purchase of a new fishing rod.

Financial advisors often ask you to create a financial policy statement that creates certain guidelines. For example, you won't put more than 10 percent in one investment class, no more than 25 percent in a single sector, and no more than 3 percent in a single security. Or you'll sell any security when it goes down 15 percent or more.

You could put that kind of thinking into a life policy statement that you work on with a partner: You won't spend more than Y on clothing and I'll keep the cost of my hobbies to X. When the account goes to a certain level, that's when we go on a trip.

However you negotiate the details, I firmly believe that whatever plan you make should take both of you—together or individually—to the finish line. Your obligation to a spouse supersedes any other.

You have to clarify your motivations, consider your obligations, and then do the calculations. Whether the economy is on the rise or it's tanking, the overall numbers and percentages taken out of context are far less important than knowing how what's going on will affect *you* and your life.

Come to Terms with Risk

My older clients, the ones who had some kind of personal connection to the Great Depression, understand that risk is real. The lessons they learned during that difficult time make them especially risk averse, fearful of being too aggressive. If our planning seems to veer too far for their comfort in either direction, they quickly put on the brakes. That attitude cuts both ways: It may save them some angst in difficult times but it also kept their capital underperforming for long stretches of time.

For the majority of people, of course, the Depression is something out of the history books—a sepia-toned image of a long-ago time when many people didn't have automobiles or flush toilets. They can't even imagine how widespread the anxiety was. People who came of age after World War II have experienced a world in which, with infrequent and brief exceptions, the financial tide just kept rising.

Those who cannot remember the past are condemned to repeat it, Santayana said. With memories of the Wall Street crash of 1929 and the subsequent upheavals fading, in 2008 the Cosmos taught younger generations a sobering lesson that, like veterans of the Depression, they may carry with them for many decades.

Americans experienced some frightening times during the 16-month recessions of 1973–1975 and 1980–1982. A lot of Rust Belt companies went under during these recessions, but the hard times deeply affected only lagging pockets of the economy, far away from much of the population.

In contrast, the meltdown that began in September 2008 affected Americans where they live—literally: Many of them lost their homes. The crisis was the result of years of low interest rates, new mortgage products, and easy lending standards that allowed people to refinance every time the value of their residences went up, in essence allowing people to use them as ATM machines.

People expected that the momentum would continue and waited for the next uptick in values to refinance and pull out more cash. But when the bubble burst, they couldn't access any more capital. Many of them owed more money than their homes were worth. They couldn't afford to keep up the mortgage payments, and the banks foreclosed.

Taking on mortgages they couldn't pay wasn't the only way in which Americans in recent decades were living beyond their means. Easy credit and low interest rates also encouraged them to take on an unprecedented amount of debt.

It has been suggested that the run-up in home values began once the women's movement gained traction and more women entered the workforce. The rule of thumb had been that a home, typically a family's biggest expense, should cost 2.5 times the household's income—and now that income was derived from two wage earners.

Home builders who were selling to first-time buyers could now build and price for much bigger budgets. This had a huge impact on the housing market and on spending patterns in general. Home prices zoomed up, fueled by two-income earners as well as retirees with significant assets accumulated in the postwar years. At market peak, in 2006, a median-priced home in areas like Oakland, CA, or Miami would have consumed more than 75 percent of the median income.*

But here's the catch: Eventually the young home buyers decided to have a family. Many women left the job force to become stay-at-home moms, and now a 30-year-old husband might be trying to pay for the house (and support the family) on a single income. Many of them found it impossible.

For a lot of young families with kids, the system took away the dream along with the house. Then they started with the blame game. But the real problem was that their vision had been flawed. They had calculated the future based on the most optimistic scenario: full employment for two wage earners. But, as John Lennon famously sang, "Life is what happens to you when you're busy making other plans."

For anyone—and especially for a person in or contemplating retirement—it's important that the plans include the notion that life happens. I call it getting real, and guidelines exist.

Lose the Hunter Mentality

When I'm dealing with couples, I notice that wives understand the kind of attitude needed for retirement planning more intuitively than their husbands. It's probably a matter of wiring. Men have been hunters and gatherers since the beginning of time. A caveman got up in the morning and announced he was going out to bag a woolly mammoth. "Great, dear," said his wife, but she'd have a backup of bark jerky just in case the game proved elusive.

---

* By 2009, it had gone back down to, respectively, 26 and 34 percent; see Jane Hodges, "First-time Buyers Benefit from Housing Slump," 5/8/09, online at www.msnbc.msn.com/id/30551169/.

Certainly in my experience, men tend to focus more on acquisition—they look at scorecards and symbols and material things—whereas women are more concerned about security and well-being. As people age, however, security and well-being become the primary mutual concern. And the recent economic environment, which kicked everyone in the teeth, led many of my clients to ask me (and themselves), "Why should I be pushing so hard to acquire more?"

Most of them come to the proper conclusion: They shouldn't. Retirement is not about having more; it's about getting to the finish line. It's not about acquisition, but management; not about taking risk, but controlling it; not about boldness, but about prudence. It's about being able to sleep at night.

Nevertheless, one quirky trend emerges in the aftermath of a setback like the one that began in 2008. Being forced to reevaluate their retirement plans, some people may be tempted to try for one last Big One.

Don't Swing for the Fences

Young people have lots of time to bounce back from someone else's malpractice or their own uninformed decisions. But older people don't. There are pills to reduce your blood pressure to normal, but there's no prescription that will get you back to your financial starting line. You may hope for doubles or triples, but you can't count on them, and you have fewer opportunities to get up at bat.

Nevertheless, sensing limited opportunity, some people near or in retirement will go after high-stakes risks. In fact, even as I was writing this chapter, a client in his late 60s forwarded a proposal from a friend "who gets in on the great deals." In this case, you put $3,500 in a "real estate deal" that in short order returns over $100,000. My client asked my opinion. I told him I thought the best part was that his loss was capped at $3,500.

At 28, chances are you have a modest amount of funds. If you take a flyer with $10,000 and it turns into $50,000, you're over the moon. But at 58, you may only get juiced by the prospect that

$50,000 will become $250,000. So you try a high-octane maneuver in hopes of a single windfall that will recoup your past losses.

If your big move fails at 28, you can shrug it off: "I've blown ten grand." But taking a hit of $50,000 at age 58 is likely to have a much greater impact on your future. A five-digit loss may require digging into your reserve tank, eliminating the cushion you might need to pay for groceries for a year or two. And you have less time to ride the market back up.

It's not unusual for people to use one excuse after another to put off making a commitment to save. "We'll do it later"—after they renovate the kitchen, or enclose the porch, or take that big trip, or buy the recreational vehicle.

Most years, you are likely to have a large, unanticipated budget item such as a dental bill, a housing repair, or a car breakdown. Over 15 or 20 years, these items may have added up to a six-figure amount that never made it into your savings fund. To play catch-up, a client may push me to make more aggressive allocations to hit one over the fence. But I push back. That's not a prudent way to prepare for the future.

Getting serious about retirement means getting real about your prospects and your strategies.

Think Goals, Not Performance

When you're building your career and amassing assets, you're all about acceleration and expansion: You're going forward and up, thinking bigger and bigger. You want the fastest jockey in the shed. *My broker can beat your broker.*

In those days, you were telling your money guy, "Get me more." We tend to run our lives in search of more. Once you sell a business, you start looking for a bigger one. Once you have had a really good car, you start looking for a better one. Once you own a great house, you're ready for one that's greater still.

Now everything is different. Retirement planning should be goals-based, not return-based.

That's a big adjustment. We're conditioned to look for returns, and returns are the lure that the financial services industry uses as bait. Of course returns are important. But you can't look at them in a vacuum. The only reason to keep chasing ever-bigger numbers is if you don't know what number you need.

Wealth Isn't a Number

If you ask people to define wealth, they often come up with a figure that's just about twice what they have. That's because people want to protect whatever they have accumulated. And twice what you actually have allows plenty of breathing room. If things collapse even 50 percent, you're back at the starting place.

Wealth isn't a number; it's a state of mind. And success? It's tranquility. People who earn $35,000 and live strictly hand to mouth, paycheck to paycheck, are used to living with a cap on their expectations. They know the limits to their lifestyle.

Contrast them with the folks who have a million-dollar business and are living a $250,000 lifestyle. They can do that by writing off their car for business reasons, covering some of their entertainment costs by dining with clients at fancy restaurants, and enjoying a getaway by extending a business trip for a couple of days. But if those folks sell the business for $1 million and put that in the bank, to be prudent, they shouldn't spend more than 5 percent, or $50,000 a year. That's a big comedown from a $250,000-a-year lifestyle.

Meanwhile, the $35,000-a-year people who retire and—between Social Security, savings, and a part-time job—can count on $35,000 a year in retirement, might wind up with a lot less anxiety. The wage earners can guarantee their lifestyle, whereas the guys coming into big money may be living beyond their true means.

Put Everything in Context

The number that is important to you is the one you need to live on in your vision of the future. There's no point getting depressed or euphoric about the size of your portfolio without any sense of the context.

For example, a woman in her mid-70s was referred to me. Her net worth had shrunk from $4 to $1.7 million in the months after September 2008. She couldn't sleep at night. She was sick to her stomach. She had no long-term plan, and I asked her to come in with a list of her expenses.

I discovered that she was living on a very modest scale. Her home was paid for, she didn't care about buying a new car until the old one absolutely had to be replaced, and she had no extravagant desires. After reviewing the numbers, I assured her that with her $1.7 million, she could do anything she wanted; that in fact, even taking inflation into effect, she could increase her expenses by 25 percent and still have enough to keep going past age 95.

This wasn't voodoo accounting on my part. I was working with easily verified facts, the ones she herself gave me. But without a plan, her security had been tied to an abstract number. When the number went up, she felt good, and when it went down, she panicked. In terms of her real situation, though, those ups and downs were irrelevant. If you need just 450 yards of wool to make a sweater, whether you have an additional 100 yards or 150 yards isn't critical to your goal.

In contrast, another woman I spoke with inherited some money in 2003, when the market began its huge run-up. She began to spend as if the double-digit gains of those few years were going to continue indefinitely. And then the clock struck 12, and the coach and coach-men turned back into a pumpkin and mice.

When we met, she said that she was concerned about her investments. Her account was steadily going down. We helped her to go through her accounts and take a good look at her bills. We helped her see that the problem wasn't with her investments but with the way she was spending. As the quip goes, she had too much month left at the end of her money. She was depleting money much faster than she had anticipated.

We took her through the uncomfortable process of budgeting. When we helped her recognize where she spent her money, she was shocked. After that reality check, she bought Quicken, a personal finance software program, and began to watch over what she was doing. She told me she's much more comfortable these days, knowing exactly what she can spend rather than turning a blind eye and hoping everything would be all right. She feels empowered and secure.

Don't Benchmark from the High

Math quiz: If you buy 100 shares of stock at $40 and a year later it's worth $80, how much profit did you make? Answer: None—unless you sell it.

That's the perspective you have to take. When the Dow fell below 7,000 in 2008, people started calculating how much they'd lost from the high. "If only I had sold everything the day the market hit 14,000!" they'd say. Or, "I'd have been in a great place if I'd gotten out." Then they'd tell you they were down 40 percent. In actual dollars, they might have been down only 10 percent, but they were looking at paper gains and losses. If you keep benchmarking from new, ever-higher perches, you'll be continually disappointed. You can't delude yourself that you own each new high. Down that road lies madness.

Getting overly euphoric when things are going well gives you a false sense of security. And the reverse is also true. Unless you lock in the gains or the losses, they don't count. What matters is what effect the highs and lows have on your world—how they affect your plan.

Live Off Your Balance Sheet

In the course of recruiting commission-based brokers in my career, I found that most guys would take their best month, multiply the commission by 12, and in their heads, that became their annual revenue. If someone produced $200,000 a year in commissions but had a $30,000 month, he'd tell me that he was a $360,000 producer. He thought he was doing a snow job on me, but he was actually conning himself— mostly, I suspect, to justify the fact that he was probably a $360,000-a-year spender, living on his potential rather than his income.

Sales managers in the brokerage business—in every business, for that matter—love to see employees ramp up their lifestyles and spend money based on next year's raise. That keeps the staff hungry. It's motivational, sure, but it's also delusional, irrational behavior. Though events may help you zoom ahead from time to time, you can't count on being in the passing lane forever.

If you do, you're probably living on debt. The translation for "low monthly payments" is "high profits for the lender." When you finance an item, you're paying for it many times over. And it's not really yours. During my childhood, one of the neighbors had all the toys: new cars, a pool, furs, and jewelry for his wife. But my father used to say, "He didn't buy any of that stuff. He's making monthly payments on it. He's just renting it."

If you own something, you can ride out the rough times. But if it's on loan, an interruption in your cash flow can be disastrous. The only place you'll be driving that leased Porsche or BMW is back to the dealer.

Certainly going into retirement is no time to be living off more income than you can reasonably expect your assets to generate.

Drop Out of the Trade-Up Generation

In April 2000, I had an epiphany that was wonderfully liberating.

A business transaction had left me flush with cash, and my first impulse was to move up to the next rung on the ladder. Instead of living in a gorgeous house, I was going to move up to an insanely gorgeous house. Though the home we were in was beautiful and met all our family's needs, now we could meet needs I had never even contemplated.

I had spent my whole life looking for the next building block to climb onto. I have the mind-set of someone always grasping for the next rung on the ladder, so much so that I started my own brokerage firm at the age of 28. And I came of age in the 1970s and 1980s, watching shows like *Dynasty*. My whole generation, the trade-up generation, was into acquisition. People were defined by their stuff and the labels that were on the stuff. Why drive a Chevy if you could drive a Cadillac? And why drive a Cadillac if you could drive a Mercedes-Benz?

Then, suddenly, it occurred to me, *What are we doing?* I was already concerned that my wife was spending too much time cleaning, and in the new house, she'd have even more to clean. The kids' friends all lived in the old neighborhood, so we'd be carpooling them back on a regular basis.

I thought back to when we moved out of our apartment and spent the first night in our house. I woke up to use the bathroom, and I realized how much further I had to walk. Now that I was older, I was waking up more often—and I was thinking of moving into a place where the bathroom would be even *further* away?

I decided to stay put.

That was a life-changing decision. And immediately afterward, a weird thing happened. For the first time in my life, I felt I had enough. I felt secure. More than that: I felt wealthy. I had a house that was paid for and a balance in my bank account that wasn't earmarked for any particular purpose.

Abandon the Bubble-and-Burst Lifestyle

If I'd had the higher mortgage when the market went to hell, I'd have been regretting the decision to trade up every day. Sure, it makes sense to expand your budget when times are great, but only within reason. Having to sell assets because the good times have stopped rolling is just not a way to head into your retirement years.

The global economic crisis that began in the fall of 2008 came because companies totally failed to evaluate how much risk they were taking. Individuals can fall into the same trap.

It's very liberating to get yourself out of a self-imposed scenario of ever-expanding-expenses. If the headlines are screaming about a financial crisis and you don't freak out because it's not going to affect your lifestyle or your goals; if your reaction is *Yeah, that's terrible, and it's going to affect me, but it's not going to crush me*—that's when you know you've done the right thing.

You're Responsible for Your Future

Whether you call on professional help to make the transition into retirement, you're the one driving the action in the story of your own life. Those ads that say, "Tell us your dreams and we'll take you anywhere," really bother me. You meet a planner, tell him your dreams, and leave it up to him to get you there in comfort and style? This is such disingenuous thinking. A financial advisor is not your travel agent or your chauffeur. He may provide help and advice to make the trip a good one, he may be your GPS system, but you're the one at the wheel. You're in charge, and it's you who makes the ultimate judgment calls.

I know a lot of people who say that when the market is down, they don't open their investment statements. This never fails to amaze me. Suppose someone's stealing your money? Suppose the statement says you have zero in the account? Knowledge is power. It arrives at your front door, and you choose not to have it?

Each of us is responsible to care for ourselves and the other inhabitants of our own world. Being in charge is a huge obligation. Inevitably, when things get messed up, we want a scapegoat. But that's just tears on the pillow.

You don't have to be self-sufficient, but you do have to be self-reliant. If there's less money in your account, it's not your advisor who's going to deal with the consequences. It's up to you to take the ultimate responsibility for your plan and be sufficiently empowered to own your decisions. It's up to you to ask the right questions and to understand how the answers apply to your particular situation. Just like it's up to you to keep to your own budget.

Be Realistic about Retirement

People think they'll spend less money in retirement, but actually the reverse may be true. Work-related budget items—business clothes, transportation to work, and similar expenses—may go down, but with more time on your hands, you may start spending more to entertain yourself: eating out, going to movies and museums, taking classes, traveling, and so on.

And there are other ways you may be spending your money: Are you contemplating educating yourself for a second career or funding a post-retirement business? Have you allowed for the possibility inflation will reduce the buying power of your dollar?

What about health insurance? If you plan to stop working at 62, how are you going to cover the medical insurance until you're eligible for Medicare? Will Medicare be kicking in later than it has in the past? How much will it cover? What will you have to pay for supplemental medical and drug insurance?

If you're not sure you've anticipated every possible stumbling block, you should consider getting outside help. People come to financial advisors like me to help them sit down and think about these things.

How Much Fuel Are You Burning?

To know whether you have enough fuel to get to the finish line, you have to start by knowing how much fuel per mile you're burning.

Tracking your spending is a horrible job. You have to do it. End of story.

Though I've said people can make a remarkably accurate guesstimate of what they have, rarely do they have a good handle on how they're spending it. Their estimates are either way high or way low, which always seems weird to me and is invariably shocking to them.

Here's a typical recent example: A client asked me to counsel her daughter, a young woman in her 20s who didn't have a clue about managing money. I started by asking her how much she spent on food. She said she spent $500 a month for groceries. But when I asked her what she spends on lunch at work, she explained that she usually ordered from the local delicatessen. That came to $10 or $12 a day. So suddenly, the $500 food budget item became more than $800.

One good way to start tracking your spending is with your credit card bill. All companies send out year-end summaries. When I looked at my own, I was blown away by what I spent at my favorite sushi restaurant. In fact, I'm wondering why the guy isn't sending me a Christmas card, at least. Someone said, "Starbucks can steal your retirement one grande frappucino at a time." Do the numbers. Five bucks a day comes to $1,500 a year; do that for 30 years, at a modest 6 percent growth rate, and that's $127,202.52.

Say you're calculating an even lower rate of return for your money—just 4 percent. To generate $6,000, you'd need $150,000. But if you cut your expenses by $500 a month, you can manage with $150,000 less in your nest egg.

Most people find that when they go through their line items, they can eliminate or substantially reduce the costs of things they won't even miss.

Budget by the Bucket

A surprising number of people don't factor into their planning big budget items looming ahead—a child's wedding, the repayment due for their share of the boat, help for the grandchildren's tuition—and just leave it to fate to provide. But unless you have a huge amount of discretionary income or you win the lottery, you won't meet these items without a plan.

The best way to do it is to set aside certain amounts as bucket funds, each in a separate account and earmarked for expenses you can anticipate—a child's college education, for example. When you look at your net worth, don't even take those funds into consideration.

If your nest egg at 52 amounts to $600,000 and if you anticipate giving your 18-year-old a $30,000 wedding down the road, that will make a pretty big impact on your retirement account. If the market's roaring, perhaps you can peel off some funds and throw them into the wedding bucket. Otherwise, when the market goes down, you have to choose: Does the wedding get reduced to a $5,000 affair in the back yard, or do you postpone your plans to retire?

one category of risk only you can handle, because it resides within your own mind. One of the biggest challenges to financial planning is that our relationship with money is not always rational.

Key Takeaways

- **Live the life you can afford.** If you want to be able to enjoy the harvest in the years ahead, you have to begin building the stores in the warehouse now. You can't rely on credit cards and next year's raise to meet your present costs of living. If you're writing IOUs that your nest egg will eventually have to make good on, you're simply stealing from your future self.

- **Consider the impact of inflation.** Whatever goods and services cost you today, the prices will go up in the future. When the market goes down, we see our investment accounts decline; when we withdraw money from the bank to buy a new car, we see our savings balance go lower. But we don't see the effect of inflation shrinking our assets in such a dramatic way, so it's easy to ignore its corrosive effect. Doing so can sabotage your retirement plans.

- **Focus on fulfilling your intentions rather than on increasing returns.** In retirement you should stop looking at the numbers to see what's going on. Instead, you should be measuring your financial progress by calculating whether you are achieving your goals on an ongoing basis. Your future security isn't determined by a number but by what you need that number to do for you.

- **Design a plan that works for you.** Just as it is impossible to put the 20th floor on a building unless you have an accurate blueprint to guide you, you can't be sure you'll be able to get where you want to twenty years in the future without factoring in all the details. Any useful plan should anticipate large, predictable future expenses such as education, a wedding, and household maintenance and also build in shock absorbers to handle unexpected issues.

- **Take control of your future.** Build your defense system: Find ways to bring in income to cover shortfalls and get rid of debt. Put your financial life in order. Assume responsibility, and call in help if you need it. Knowing that you've anticipated and planned for what lies down the road will help you stick to your plan.

3

Dump the Head Trash

THE QUESTION I'M ASKED most is the one that matters least:

"How did the market do today?"

For anyone planning retirement, this is very much beside the point. Here's the only question that matters:

"How are *you* doing today?"

What's important is not how the market is reacting but how you're reacting to the market. Your perception determines how you respond to the inevitable stresses of changing conditions and how diligently you will stick to your goals to make it to the finish line.

I am convinced that your attitude about money is the single most important factor that determines the course of your financial future.

You and Your Money

There are two ways to create wealth. One is by saving it—stockpiling whatever is left over after you've taken care of your needs. The other is by investing it—putting it at risk in hopes that it will grow. The majority of people can't put aside enough excess cash to rely on savings as their major retirement resource, so at some point in their life they must become investors. Entrepreneurs create their own companies to invest in; nonentrepreneurs can participate in ownership via the stock market.

Investing always involves risk and uncertainty, and those factors engage your emotions. How you respond to your emotions depends on how you're wired. People tend to believe that how they personally deal with money issues is pretty much the same as how everyone else does, but that's not so.

When the market's down, I field calls from some anxious clients, the ones who are ready to jump into the bunkers. They want reassurance, and they assume that's universally true. "You must be getting crushed by calls like these," they'll often say, and they're shocked to learn that I'm not. It's unfathomable to them that someone is out on the golf course or ordering twin lobster meals while they're preparing for doomsday.

I hear less frequently from the other kind of clients, the ones who like to believe that everything will eventually take care of itself. These people are generally incredulous to learn that some people call daily: "What do they hope to achieve by that? What a waste of time!" When I reach out to clients like these even to make a routine appointment to discuss their accounts, typically the response is, "Why do I need to worry about any of this? That's what you're there for."

If you're the worrying type, you'll probably overreact to every movement of the market. And if you're someone who lets things roll off your back because you're a born optimist, you're likely to ignore warning signs and fail to act at all. Recognizing how your temperament may bias your decision making is every bit as critical as honing your strategic investment skills.

Risk Tolerance Isn't Fixed

The most widespread—and to me, misguided—first step in dealing with individual investors is to zero in on their risk tolerance. Wall Street has trained everyone to think that risk is an investor's major concern. But this all starts with a false assumption: that risk tolerance is fixed.

After you get a big raise, you probably feel flush: You might take on more risk. But after your last three investments have gone down, you are probably less inclined to take a chance with a fourth. Your risk tolerance is more linked to how you feel about what's going on *right now* than what you think is going to happen in the future. So what you decide to do next is going to be determined by what's happened already.

Nevertheless, as soon as you sign up with an asset manager, you are always given a risk tolerance questionnaire. On Wall Street, unfortunately, the questionnaire is designed to let the firm know, *How much loss can you take before you sue?* It is often thrown back in a client's face after a time of great volatility: *Look*, the firms say, *you signed this. Remember? You said you felt comfortable with volatility.*

In fact, I don't think risk tolerance itself is a big issue. People are accustomed to taking risks. They take them every time they take a new job, get married—or eat in a restaurant, for that matter.

What drives us are our primitive impulses: fear and greed, the instinct to hoard versus the instinct to hunt. Most people aren't on an extreme end of the scale but rather tend to lean one way or another. When the market is rip-roaring, hoarders second-guess themselves because they're getting low returns and the hunters are flying high. When the market is on a downward trend, the hunters lose their certitude and retreat to safety.

I find that it's indeed a truism that people are long-term investors as long as they're making money in the short term. When the market's going up, people will take more risk because they perceive they'll make more. When it's going down, they'll take less.

On that questionnaire you filled out, you may have said you wanted aggressive growth, but when the market's on the decline, you may change your preference to conservative income production. I myself ask clients to fill out a risk tolerance questionnaire, but not to nail down attitudes they will have to live with for the next 10 years. Instead, I use it to help clients recognize that their risk tolerance is not fixed. The loss of money, in my opinion, is not what really distresses them.

An Investor's Worst Fear

What really bothers people is very simple. *They just don't want to make a mistake.*

After all, not all risk can be viewed from a downside perspective. It's important to understand the distinction between risk and volatility. Volatility means up and down movement of the market, something over which the investor has no control. On the other hand, risk is about making the wrong decision. Knowing they have the power—and that they've misused it—is what makes people crazy.

Example: Suppose that a broker advises his client to buy XYZ at 2, then recommends selling it at 4. At the time, the client is delighted to have made a 100 percent profit. But if a week later, XYZ goes to 8, you can be sure he or she is no longer so happy.

Having dealt with the public as an executive in the financial services industry for so many years, I am amazed to remember how few complaints I got when a broker recommended buying a stock that went down and, in contrast, how many I got when a broker recommended selling a stock that subsequently went up—not a year later, but within the following week, or day.

Risk aversion isn't fixed. But loss aversion is. No one wants to lose.

Here's another example: Suppose you're one of a group of 30 people, each of whom buys a lottery ticket. Each of you puts your initials on the one you've purchased, and then you swap them around. On jackpot day, the ticket you're holding doesn't win, but the one you initialed—now held by someone else—pays off. If the ticket had originally been purchased by that other person, you'd probably shrug off the incident. But the fact that you once held the winner and then gave it up creates remorse.

And if the magnitude of the loss is great—if your portfolio sinks to the point where you may lose your lifestyle—the pain of losing something you once had can be unbearable. What's more, that's true in equal measure whatever the lifestyle you're letting go of—whether it's one that includes mansions and a private jet or a trailer home and a rusty pickup truck.

Aversion to loss—even when it creates irrational behavior—overrides every other investment consideration.

Instead of trying to define a client through asking about risk tolerance, a financial counselor should ask, "If you had X amount less money, how would it affect you, both literally and emotionally?"

Your Psyche Is Ground Zero

The Phoenix Affluent Marketing Service estimated in June 2009 that the number of millionaire households had fallen to 5.1 million, which according to its figures, was a drop of 14 percent in two years.*

Everyone was looking to place the blame. When you see your money evaporate, it's human nature to want to point the finger at some person or some external cause. But sometimes the finger has to point right back at you.

As your own wealth manager, you have to answer to yourself. You need to ask in what ways your thinking, and your subsequent actions, have contributed to any problems you might have. Whatever you learn from past experience makes you less vulnerable in the future.

The most important investment you can make is the time you spend understanding who you are financially. To protect your nest egg, you have to understand your own, individual relationship to money. In the process, your psyche becomes ground zero.

We make our biggest mistakes when we are confronted with uncertainty, and risk and uncertainty are built into the process of investing. One key to surviving uncertainty is preparation. Before a passenger ship leaves port, it does a muster drill. All the passengers are summoned on board, asked to put on life vests, and told to gather near the lifeboats.

---

*Online at phoenixmi.com.

By envisioning the worst-case scenario and doing a run-through of the preparations, you have a plan of action should a disaster become reality. That's how SWAT teams get ready. They have the same adrenalin rush as other humans in an emergency situation but they can function efficiently because they've anticipated the most probable scenarios and have a response prepared.

As an investor, you have to do likewise.

So Many Smart People, So Many Dumb Mistakes

Every investor has made an irrational move. Somebody gives you five hot tips, you lose on all of them, and then the same guy calls and you take the bait for a sixth. Or instead of getting out of a poor investment with a small loss, you hold on and wind up with a big one.

The reasons why such behavior is so commonplace and so many very smart people make so many dumb mistakes have all been explored by scientists working in a relatively new discipline called behavioral economics. It investigates the link between psychology and economics, particularly regarding judgment and decision making in uncertain conditions.

Social scientists have observed that not only individuals but also entire groups can react for reasons that are emotional rather than rational, which is why sometimes the movement of markets defies any logical explanation.

Many of the observations that behavioral scientists write about seem to be simply a matter of common sense. But it can be a real eye-opener to find yourself following some of the patterns of irrational thinking that they describe.

Since the likelihood of your making it to the finish line depends— more than anything else—on how you think about your money, you need to remove the head trash to stay purposeful and steady. First you have to know what it is, and how it's expressed. In my years as a financial advisor, I've learned that head trash comes in a variety of categories.

Trash Thinking Category # 1: Acting Impulsively

"I'm going with my gut."

Translation: I don't want to think about this any more.

I personally am very reliant on my gut. Where someone else might just see a few extra pounds, I see a warehouse for ideas. I'm only half joking. You are not born with a gut, either literally or (more important here) figuratively. You develop it over time. Thinking with your gut definitely qualifies as "thinking," because your gut contains and processes data you've acquired over the years.

Here's a great example: In 1949, in Montana's Mann Gulch River Valley, there was a ferocious fire. Fifteen firefighters parachuted in to help fight it. They were heading downhill to cross a river and reach the blaze when suddenly the wind blew it right at them. Instinctively, they started running away. Though Wagner Dodge, their leader, ordered them to stand still, most ignored what seemed like an absurd command.

But Dodge realized that they couldn't possibly outrun the flames, and in an instant his gut helped him come up with the idea of an "escape fire": Burn the area in front of you to clear it of vegetation, lie down, and wait for the fire (which will now have no fuel) to pass over you. Following that plan, Dodge and one other firefighter were the only survivors. The point is, Dodge had enough experience that his gut was an educated and reliable guide, and he allowed it to override his instinct.

Certainly, acting instinctively can have merit. Our built-in survival responses protect us from dangers and emergencies. If some sixth sense makes you feel uncomfortable about the person who sits next to you in a subway car, it's appropriate to move elsewhere. But if *everyone* sitting near you in a subway car makes you uncomfortable, then your warning system isn't to be trusted.

When you see the whole system as dangerous or hopeless and react with panic and depression, that's not thinking with your gut. That's paranoia. Groundless and irrational emotions shouldn't guide your decision.

Remember also that when our primal selves saw danger, it was coming in real time and we had to react immediately. If the saber-toothed tiger charged and you didn't run, you were dead. But the financial world is virtual. The market surges on hope and goes down on apprehension. It's about perception more than reality, and the perceptions are priced daily.

By the time the real world is acting in the way we're defending against, our reactions are inappropriate—that is, we flee the market when we should be in and vice versa. So your response to threats should be calculated rather than emotional. Rather than reacting to the accumulated events of the past, you need to be thinking where things are headed in the future, and that's when you can rely on your gut and its accumulated experience.

"I can't just do nothing."
Translation: My emotions, not my goals, are driving me.

Often, the best response to market volatility is no response. Case in point: I had a client who sold off an entire portfolio when the market took a dive. The account consisted of holdings his siblings and he would eventually inherit from their mother. She was well taken care of, and the siblings had no immediate use for the funds. In fact, when he first came to us with his account, the client had specifically asked us to invest for the long term, in view of the fact that the funds were to be used by future generations.

We made a point of explaining that such a strategy would involve more volatility than one that was meant to harvest cash in the short term, and he said he understood and agreed to take that approach.

But once the events of September 2008 started to unfold, all his intentions went out the window. Eventually, he panicked about seeing his inheritance disappear and sold everything: He turned it all into cash. Then, when the market reversed course, he watched it climb and counted the money he didn't make, which made him feel stupid on a daily basis. The only thing that might have made him happy was if the market had declined much further after he'd gotten out.

His decision to get out was driven more by his short-term emotion than his long-term goals. By doing something, you may achieve nothing.

Remember this: Once you deconstruct a rational decision with emotional actions, it's hard to construct rationality again.

"Lock in the profit."
Translation: I want it now.

In their 1998 study, "Predicting Hunger: The Effects of Appetite and Delay on Choice," researchers Daniel Read and Barbara van Leeuwen conducted a classic behavioral economics study about making choices. They asked participants to choose what dessert they'd like for a dinner next week: fruit or chocolate. About 74 percent chose the fruit.

Then the researchers asked which dessert participants would like for lunch today. In that case, 70 percent chose the chocolate. The desire for instant gratification trumps the choice we know would be more beneficial.

This also explains why people buy items they can't afford on credit, knowing they'll pay high interest on the balance.

For the same reason, people will take a small, short-term profit rather than let an investment mature. And they'll do it even though the quicker sale will trigger more taxes. Immediate gratification is a powerful motivator.

Trash Thinking Category #2: Making It All About You

"I should have seen this coming."
Translation: My magic powers should have told me when to get in (out).

No one can time the markets, but that doesn't stop people from beating up on themselves when they fail to get out before a slide or get in before a run-up.

"I like the way this guy thinks."
Translation: Since this guy thinks like I do, he must be right.

Seeking affirmation rather than information is an ineffective way to do research, but that rarely dissuades us from seeking out whatever supports our biased expectations and discounting whatever does not. People often bolster their argument for a particular position by sending me an article that contains a single point in support of their belief—and they do this even if the overall article puts forth a completely contrary point of view.

"I'll get out when I can get even."
Translation: I'm waiting until the stock gets to the number that matters to me.

In an attempt to save their self-esteem and convince themselves that they got out whole, people frequently wait for a losing stock to return to the price they paid before they unload it, in complete disregard of the fact that the particular number has significance only to them.

This thinking isn't confined to the market. A friend of mine had to move for a career opportunity but couldn't get the asking price for his home. So he took it off the market to wait until he thought he could get "the right price," an arbitrary number that met his need to reimburse himself. He couldn't focus on what was really important: selling the house in order to make a career and lifestyle change. Instead, he fixated on a single number and made his life hostage to the market. In effect, the tail wagged the dog.

In 2009, people continued to remember the portfolio total listed on their account statements when the market reached its 2007 highs. When it declined, they benchmarked to that phantom growth and bemoaned their losses. But they didn't lose the money because they never had it. If you didn't sell and realize the profit, it was never yours.

Another way to look at it: Imagine the Money Fairy appeared to you and said, *Give me your money and in return, you'll get a 6 percent annualized return in 10 years*—exactly what you need to fund the retirement lifestyle you want. In 10 years, all happens as promised, and you'd be extremely happy. Extremely happy, that is, unless you discovered someone else got a visit from the 10 percent Money Fairy.

Here's my point. Are you really off your long-term plan, or are you simply benchmarking to the highest number? That's like obsessing over the one that got away or how badly you're doing compared to Warren Buffett.

Trash Thinking Category #3: Letting Anxiety Trump Reason

"What if it goes lower?"

Translation: I'm going to lose it all.

Retirement planning is meant to help you think through the next twenty years in a rational way. But the very exercise of planning may bring all the anxiety into the present.

Don't confuse real anxiety with anticipatory anxiety. I have a lot of wealthy clients who were living in the future as paupers when the market was in its deepest slump. They mentally anticipated a freefall, with the market losing so many points a day that in no time their portfolios would go straight to zero.

You may be losing money on paper, but you have to ask yourself what's real. Extrapolating future disaster is just as senseless as extrapolating never-ending upward growth. Just as you don't have profits until you actually sell a stock, you don't have losses until you've locked them in with a sale.

"I'm too old to take any risk."

Translation: I'm ignoring the fact that I may have to fund many more years.

You used to be told to apportion your portfolio into percentages based on your age, with an increasingly larger percentage devoted to more conservative investments over time. At 50, you were supposed to be equally invested in stocks and bonds; at 60, the appropriate mix would become 60 percent bonds and 40 percent stocks; and at 70, the split would be 70–30. That was fine when most people died in their 70s, but without exposure to the growth that historically comes from investing in equities, most people will find it difficult to fund the life expectancies that we anticipate today.

Jeff Bezos was 30 when he began to look for venture capital to start an online bookstore. His stepfather and his mother, who was only 47, invested a large portion of their life savings into what became

Amazon.com. Had Jeff Bezos' mother been 67 rather than 47 when he asked her to invest, the company might never have seen the light of day.

While, as I have noted, some people approaching retirement make one last attempt to swing for the fences, most tend to become more conservative. At retirement age, you're not likely to gamble with your life savings even to fund your son's business. And you shouldn't. You need stability, not excitement.

On the other hand, the pendulum can overswing. An excess of caution is one psychological roadblock that can hijack your ability to protect your nest egg effectively. Adding stocks to diversify a portfolio of cash and bonds will almost certainly boost returns over the long run as it has historically.

Trash Thinking Category #4: Confusing the Possible and the Probable

"How could I not take a shot on that?"

Translation: This investment is so alluring I don't need the facts.

Research shows that your brain tends to have an easier time focusing on the reward rather than on the chance that you'll get it. You respond more positively to a bigger prize no matter what your odds are of winning it. That's why lottery ticket sales go way up when the jackpot is larger.

Many hedge funds are known as the "black boxes" of investment categories because they offer investors little or no information about their tactics or holdings; perversely, the secrecy is what lets them get away with charging such high fees and makes the prospect of hitting the jackpot more irresistible. Christmas wouldn't be as much fun to a kid if all the presents under the tree were in transparent boxes.

Even otherwise conservative investors, people who pride themselves on not taking big chances, respond to the powerful allure of hedge funds. Because so many have had astronomical returns, they appeal to everyone's greed. And they have the allure of a sort of club mentality. An investor is "in on" the hedge fund's confidential strategies—the attraction that lures so many to Ponzi scheme operators like Bernie Madoff.

They remove the cushion against further losses and deplete their assets by $5,000 at the same time.

Trash Thinking Category #7: Losing Perspective

"Look at what's happened to my portfolio."

Translation: The dollar amount in my portfolio shows if I'm rich or poor.

Suppose you put 1 percent of your money in a single stock that goes down to zero. Now, suppose your entire portfolio goes down 1 percent. Though the net effect in both of these scenarios is exactly the same, people view the former as a tragedy and the latter as normal fluctuation.

An even more meaningful example: Suppose you make a 5 percent return on your portfolio, and inflation is at 3 percent. Now suppose that you make a 3 percent return, and inflation is at zero. In the second example, your buying power increases by 3 percent, and in the first, by only 2 percent.

Yet most people prefer the first example because they're wrongly focused on the asset value—the higher number. But it's the buying power that matters. The only value money has is what you can exchange it for.

When people compute their worth, they tend to focus on the market to the exclusion of their other holdings. Because Wall Street is priced every day, what goes on there affects our psyche and ability to stay the course, yet you should be looking at your whole financial picture. (How differently would you view your finances if the value of every single thing you owned was repriced daily?)

"The market closed where?"

Translation: Only today matters.

Everyone was gleeful when the market hit 10,000 for the first time in 1999. But when it reached 10,000 in 2008, there was universal depression, since it was retreating from a high of 14,000. When it reached 10,000 in October 2009—up from the low of 6,443 in March—that was "breaking news" on TV, and the media covered the milestone with all the hoopla of New Year's Eve. Same number, different perspectives.

The lens through which you see something determines the action you will take, a phenomenon known to behavior economists as framing. When you see an issue from only one perspective, you can delude yourself by maximizing or minimizing other factors, and your subsequent decisions may be faulty.

Trash Thinking Category # 8: Being Committed to Commitment

"I know this stock."

"This stock is my baby."

"I might not buy more at this price, but I wouldn't sell it at this price, either."

Translation: Breaking up is hard to do.

Behavioral scientists explain that the act of commitment raises our confidence in an outcome, no matter what the odds are for or against it. Many people have a long-term relationship with a particular issue. Fall in love with a significant other, with your children, or your baseball team—but not with your stocks.

"I hate to lose money."

Translation: Anything is possible.

People hang onto a losing equity even when all the indicators are negative and the prospects for the future seem hopeless—yet another demonstration of loss aversion. Although I've said it's not a loss until you sell it, if the chances of its coming back are so remote as to be a fantasy, you have to let go.

Be Guided by Your Goals

Being put through a stress test of a volatile market no doubt showed you how easy it is to be whipsawed by current events. The natural inclination to react emotionally, which comes in many permutations, can be overridden only if you have insight into your investment temperament; if you recognize when you're making decisions based on instinct rather than facts; and if you're goals based.

Being goals-based makes you less vulnerable not only to internal pressures but also to external pressures—the flood of information and advice aimed at today's investor.

Key Takeaways

- **Don't let emotions call the shots.** Making rash, impulsive, adrenaline-fueled decisions rather than basing your actions on unimpassioned, careful deliberations will have a more catastrophic effect on your financial future than any specific portfolio choice. The most important investment skill that you can acquire is learning to manage your perceptions and reactions to the periodic and inevitable market ups and downs.
- **Realize that loss aversion, not risk tolerance, drives most investment choices.** Investment advisors usually begin by asking about your risk tolerance, which pigeon-holes you as an "aggressive" or a "conservative" investor. But risk tolerance isn't fixed. If you're feeling flush because you've had a windfall or the market is riding high, you'll probably be more inclined to take larger risks, while during the periods when the market's in the doldrums, you'll be more risk averse. People don't mind taking risks, but people do mind losing money.
- **Make your decisions based on research and knowledge.** There is no point in waiting for a buy or sell opportunity based on some idiosyncratic personal benchmark. There is no reason to fall for a sales pitch just because the seller is someone whose thinking is usually in line with yours. There is no logic to fleeing out of the market or investing in a particular sector because everyone else is. Have solid reasons for making the choices you do.
- **Don't jump to extreme conclusions.** Deciding that you can't afford any kind of risk is just as irrational as putting your money into some long shot in a desperate attempt to make up some losses. Assuming you're going to lose every penny when the market goes into a decline is just as misguided as believing that rising markets will continue ever upward.

public relations divisions that pursue the press; and, of course, so do corporations and small businesses.

Consider the Source

Stories generated by public relations people can't be blatantly dishonest. If caught in a lie, any of them would be fired and their firms wouldn't stay in business. Still, public relations specialists want the news to reflect the point of view they are supporting, and they can take advantage of the fact that most media today don't have the resources to expand or dig down into every story.

While staffers at the *Wall Street Journal* and the *New York Times* are unlikely to rely exclusively on the information presented in press releases, elsewhere, if reporters get a story from a public relations firm they trust, they may run it as a news story without even editing it.

What they get may be stories that are true, but selectively so—containing only facts that are favorable to a client and omitting others that are not. Or the stories, though not flat-out duplicitous, may be a little free and easy with the facts.

In the early years of online marketing, a startup company that offered a service for online retailers estimated there were roughly 5,000 such retailers and relayed this figure in a press release. Once one publication reported this number in print, so did others, and soon it became the accepted wisdom. Everyone "knew" there were 5,000 online retailers.

Then, the startup, which had 1,000 clients, could claim that it was serving 20 percent of online retailers. It had the 1,000 clients, but whether that group represented one-fifth of all online retailers—well, that wasn't necessarily so.

Since public relations is less expensive than advertising, some startups may put their whole marketing budget into it, hoping to get positive news stories that will drive up their stock prices.

Reporters often subscribe to newsletters to stay abreast of developments in a variety of areas. Because newsletters can be produced on a very limited budget, they are easily created by individuals and organizations promoting a particular point of view. If a reporter relies on the newsletter as the only source of news or commentary because a dwindling budget doesn't allow for in-depth reporting, what appears in print may not be a balanced story.

The producers and editors who put together print and broadcast news always look for experts willing to comment on the featured story. But they may be inclined to interview mainly (or only) sources who will corroborate their key points. For example, if based on some preliminary reporting, a producer has decided to do a story that pharmaceuticals are a hot investment opportunity right now or that commodities will be slumping, the producer will book speakers who will support that notion.

As the person most responsible for safeguarding your own financial future, it's up to you to know when you're hearing facts and when you're hearing an opinion. It's one thing to let a gecko in an ad charm you into purchasing car insurance and another to assemble your portfolio under the influence of hidden persuaders.

I am not suggesting there is anything diabolical or even deliberately misleading about the vast majority of these practices. I myself have often appeared on news broadcasts and written articles to comment on the news in hopes that the opportunity will allow me to make a favorable public impression for my company and its services. But as an investor charged with protecting your own interests, it's up to you to bear in mind that reporters and producers are not your financial advisors, to recognize that what you hear may be self-serving, and to be aware of the limits of the media's usefulness.

Coverage May Be Superficial

Though the newspapers and broadcasters bemoan the cutbacks that have shrunk their reporting staffs, a station down South managed to send out a crew to cover the story of a leprechaun spotted in a tree and one in the Northwest documented the story of a cat burglar who stole items from clotheslines and turned out to be, in fact, a cat.

But where were the investigative reporters from the financial press over the past several years, when two of the biggest business-page stories of the decade were developing? In the case of the credit default catastrophe and the Ponzi scheme perpetuated by Bernie Madoff, the real reporting didn't happen until the horse had already left the barn.

As a former chairman of the NASDAQ stock exchange, Madoff was certainly known to the press. There was a certain secretiveness and mystique about Madoff's operation, but in the closed and clannish world in which he moved, that wasn't unique.

A couple of individuals tried to sound the alarm on his business practices that provoked some federal Securities and Exchange Commission (SEC) investigations, but once the SEC concluded that there was nothing to investigate, the media didn't pursue the story. And none of them sniffed any smoke, though Madoff's unparalleled record of large and steady returns—even in years when the market was underperforming—was odd, at the very least.

His reputation insulated Bernie Madoff from scrutiny. Up until December 11, 2008, he doesn't seem to have been the subject of major investigative reporting—or any reporting at all. It was only after December 12, the day he made his startling confession of fraud on a monumental scale, that the press finally scrambled to find out what was going on.

That's typical, I think. Certainly when it comes to investing—the subject I know best and follow most closely—I find that the media shine light only on the surface of stories. They don't feel the obligation or may not have the resources to try to figure out where things are going. They tell you what happened. They investigate—but only after the fact.

Perhaps the problem is that the majority of journalists and broadcasters are trained just as journalists and broadcasters—not as financial specialists or historians or scientists. They move from beat to beat but don't have deep background in the areas they cover.

Besides, their employers, the publishers and the station owners, don't have the same goals as the readers and viewers. While the latter want information, the former want an audience. They're businessmen whose purpose is to sell advertising. The way to stay ahead in the media business is to attract the most eyeballs. That means featuring the most exciting story—and, preferably, being first to do so. The problem is that just because it's a headline doesn't mean it's important. And vice versa.

Everything's Not Black or White

The development of 24/7 news coverage has added another element to "noise"—the speed at which it's delivered.

The sense of urgency, the perception that you have do something *right now*, is heightened when a broadcast producer adds a count-down clock at the bottom of the screen. You get the same adrenaline rush as in the James Bond movies when the clock on the doomsday device begins ticking.

Moments after any headline that might impact the stock markets flashes across the TV screen or updates are sent over handheld computers, I sometimes get calls from clients anxious about whether they should respond by making changes in their portfolio.

I remind them that headlines reduce issues to black and white, and they are calculated to be provocative. As investors, what they should really keep in mind is that there is a difference between hearing "breaking news" and gaining insight into it.

As an example, when the first plane flew into the World Trade Center on 9/11, commentators thought it was just the worst aviation disaster in U.S. history. When the second plane slammed into the second tower, 15 minutes later, I heard one reporter speculate that the air traffic controller system was malfunctioning. To make sense of news events, you need to take the long view.

At the end of a show on the food channel, you've learned how to make a casserole. When a segment on the weather channel is over, you know if you should take an umbrella. If you're watching a drama or a sitcom, the case is solved or the confusion is resolved by the time the credits roll.

Sometimes, a financial reporter makes an attempt to summarize the business story of the day in just such a neat package. The show reports a company's earnings, experts are invited to comment, and then the host says to the expert, "So, Bob: Is that a buy, sell, or a hold?"

Here's *my* expert advice. No matter what Bob (or his counterpart) says—ignore it. You can't plan your future on sound bites. Whatever you learn from a business report should be just a starting point where you begin your fact-finding and questioning—not just about the particular company that was profiled, but how that company is representative of what's going on in its sector, how that sector fits into the global economy, and so on and so forth.

That show should simply be the impetus for doing further research or working with a professional to see how and if your portfolio should change.

Don't Let Noise Guide Your Choices

Television is still generally the main source of news for most people these days. In accordance with the old axiom for TV news programming—"If it bleeds, it leads"—financial news often distorts reality by playing up the bad news. Teasers that say, "Stocks plunge 3 percent!" are calculated to attract viewers. And—as another attention-getter—a lot of material is edited down to sound bites that are often taken out of context.

What commands attention is change. Rather than interview an analyst who makes a once-yearly prediction about a company, the media wants someone who'll comment on what's happening this week or—even better—what happened today. Remember that the long-term analyst has something substantial to impart about risk, while the commentator who takes the market's temperature frequently is just analyzing volatility. The sentiment of the day is irrelevant in the long run, even though it attracts viewers and fills up hours of programming.

Listening to the noise can be very detrimental to an investor. No matter what you hear, you may feel the need to be reactive—to do something—because noise makes you think that things are happening much faster than they are. But acting impetuously may be contrary to your interest.

The noise is not an accurate guide for decision making. The current direction of the market is not a gauge of risk. While the pundits are declaring that the sky is falling or that the Dow is on the upswing, the factors that cause stocks to go up or down are in independent motion.

Being distracted by the noise costs you a lot. You can rack up commissions by churning your account in anxiety-induced trades. You may lose opportunities to buy, and, worse, you may get shafted when you sell. By trading on noise, you're trading with the herd. If there's a stampede to unload a stock, the pace of selling may become so frantic, and you may have joined the line so late, that your sell order isn't executed at the price you were anticipating.

Vet Your Information

Along with traditional "industrial" media, such as radio, TV, and newspapers, the new "social" media—have had a huge impact on all kinds of communication and, as a result, on business. The category includes online forums, blogs, e-mail, Twitter, Facebook, and the like. And with the ubiquity of cell phones, of which a large percentage can connect to the Internet, a huge majority of the U.S. population is connected virtually all the time.

Technology not only has increased the opportunities and resources for investors but also increased the risks. Information is easier and faster to access, but in addition you're on your own to determine whether it's accurate and relevant.

What all social media have in common is that anyone can establish his own domain inexpensively, privately, and independent of any oversight. Many web sites have no governance. Anonymous sources offer advice in chat rooms. "Civilian journalists" without credentials operate as reporters. And anything-goes messaging on Facebook and Twitter spreads rumor and fact like wildfire and without differentiating between the two. It's like the wild, wild West of information exchange.

Who's responsible for this material? What are their credentials? Authenticating the information you get online—even determining the authorship of a message or sponsor of a web site—is frequently difficult. It may even be impossible to determine whether what you're reading was posted yesterday or a decade ago.

Friends might forward an e-mail warning of an impending virus attack or delivering other "news" calculated to dismay or shock. If you search a suspected phrase plus the word "hoax," you can find many sites that can separate fact from fiction, and you may discover that the e-mail in question not only is inaccurate, but also has been circulating for many years. The Internet can be a terrific tool, but *caveat lector*: Let the reader beware. You have to do your homework.

Even if a web site has timely information and commentary, it may be one-sided. Like minds come together not only in the real world but also in the virtual one. If you go into a chat room where everyone is convinced that it's time to buy gold, your suspicion that it might be time to buy gold can harden into a certainty. Even if it is a good idea, it may be inappropriate for your needs, but the din may be so over-whelming that you get swept up and move with the tide.

A lot of people seek information online through discussion groups where investors can communicate and share information. Generally, the way those work is that one person posts a comment and others respond in a sequence of add-on postings known as "threads." But you don't always know whether the information is reliable.

"Experts" who used to send newsletters via snail mail can communicate more cheaply and quickly via e-mail or a web site. The authors may be paid in cash or stock to unabashedly promote a particular company. That's perfectly legal, provided there is full disclosure about the relationship: who paid the author, how much, and in what form. But the disclosure may not be posted prominently—or at all. Obviously, a writer who is paid in stock stands to profit by driving up the share price through innuendo or outright falsehoods.

Another hitch is that people can hide behind screen names on the Internet. A single individual can post multiple fraudulent messages. Someone who wants to see a stock rise can spread the word that spectacular news is pending. Anonymous messaging can also create the illusion that some thinly traded stock is piquing the interest of a sizable number of investors.

On the other hand, there are people who want to drive a stock price down. Those are the people who short stocks, which means "borrowing" stock to sell it at a high price, in hopes that you will be able to replace it by buying it back at a lower price. To move the stock downward may be a simple matter of circulating electronic rumors that a product is flawed or a company may be facing litigation.

Back in the 1990s, the SEC recognized that investors could be duped by not knowing whether noise is being generated by hundreds of people or a single individual pretending to be hundreds. Just as police troll for child predators in chat rooms, they started monitoring chat rooms to look for financial con artists. In one case, they found a single broker using 16 different names, all supporting a particular recommendation. But they can't catch them all.

While your computer can be an excellent resource for doing homework and implementing investment strategies, you're well advised to place this warning sign above your monitor as a reminder: "Handle with Care: Potential Weapon of Financial Self-Destruction."

Filtering the Noise

One of the benefits of the information explosion is that the proliferation of resources makes it possible to learn about virtually any aspect of investing, often for little or no cost. But there's no freedom without responsibility. Your obligation is to be certain that the sources you're consulting can be trusted. Here are ways to ensure that you're getting reliable, unbiased information online or from media in general.

Don't Assume That the First Listed Is the Most Reliable

"Web optimization" specialists have ways to influence the position of sites that pop up via Internet searches. While search engines such as Google clearly label "sponsored links"—the ads at the very top of search page results—other, presumably neutral sites may have paid substantial sums to "optimize" their position and ensure that they come up in the top 10 or 20 results. You may need to go to a fourth, fifth, or sixth page before you find unbiased, academic, "non-optimized" answers.

Establish Criteria to Judge the Credibility of a Web Site

Does the web site you are consulting identify its author, indicate his or her qualifications, reveal the sponsor of the page, and indicate how to get in touch? The letters .edu (for an educational institution) or .gov (for a government organization) in the domain name may also (but not always) lend credibility. If there is no obvious date on the site, click on some of the links and see if they lead you to information that is timely. Some browsers, like Google and Yahoo!, let you conduct "news" searches that will lead you to the most recent news on a topic.

Some other things you might check:

■ Is there a ~ or % sign in the web address? Those are indicators that the page is a personal one rather than from some institution.

■ Is there an e-mail address or other means of making contact?

■ If the information cites another source, have you checked that the citation is accurate and that the other source seems credible?

■ The Internet Corporation for Assigned Name and Numbers (ICANN) authorizes registrars—the organizations that can license sites. Go to NetworkSolutions.com or Better-whosis.com, two of the larger and better established registrars, and you may be able to find out something about the site, such as how long it's been established and in whose name.

■ Look up the title or publisher of the page in a reputable directory that evaluates site contents. Two of the more reliable ones are Librarians' Index (lii.com), a publicly funded source of information about web sites, and infomine (infomine.ucr.edu), a resource of web information maintained by the University of California.

Be aware, too, that how you ask a question in large measure determines the answer you will receive. If you are thinking about investing in commodities and ask, *Is this a good time to invest in commodities?*, a search engine will most likely direct you to web sites where you will find comments from people who are bullish on the virtues of commodities.

Suppose, however, you recast that same basic question. Ask *Are commodities prices likely to move lower?* and you are likely to be directed to web sites populated by the commodity bears who believe commodities are a terrible buy. Ask your core question in several ways to compare the answers that you get.

Assume that any proprietary web site—that is, any web site with a sponsor—has an agenda. To a hammer, everything looks like a nail. That is, if you're trying to get information about annuities and you go to the web site of an insurance company, expect that they're going to push annuities. If you start asking about refinancing your mortgage and go onto the web sites of lenders, they'll make the deals look attractive no matter where the market is. Depending on what page you open on the Franklin Mint web site, you may be persuaded there are opportunities in collecting mini precision die-cast cars or acquiring the complete set of all 50 state quarters. Your best bet? Search several sites to find opposing opinions that will help you make a choice.

Don't Seek Only Affirmation

Believing that simply because someone thinks like you do, he or she must be right is head trash, yet it's human nature to give credence to a source that confirms our beliefs. It makes us feel smarter: *Aha! Did you hear what that person said? That's just what I've been saying!*

Learning that a savvy investor or strategist is putting money into a company you already own contributes to what behavioral economics call a *confirming bias,* which may influence your investing decision, just as information gathered from web sites, newsletters, or broadcasts that mirror your thinking can convince you you're right.

But it's equally important—maybe even more so—to pay attention to information that isn't so welcome. One of my clients stopped reading a well-respected columnist just because the man's position diverged from his own. Another dropped his subscription to a newsletter in 2007 when the editor got too bearish for his tastes. Those clients wanted to hear only a reflection of what they wanted to believe, even at the expense of reality.

Audiences have demonstrated that they prefer to watch the "opinion networks"—broadcast entities that take a particular perspective rather than striving to be objective. As a result, there's something out there for every taste, from the Euphoria Channel to the Scared Witless Network, each of them staffed by pundits whose choices of questions and of guests are in accordance with the station's party line.

Make it a point to listen not only to the network that makes you feel good about your opinion but also the one that drives up your blood pressure. If you're an MSNBC person, check out what they're saying on FOX News regularly, and vice versa. You need dissent to give you balance. If nothing else, hearing what the other side has to say forces you to clarify your own point of view.

Don't Be Seduced by the Poll Dances

Having to fill 24 hours of programming, all-news stations face the prospect of running out of news. So they've figured out how to manufacture some of their own. They call it "polling." They commission polls about investment trends, consumer sentiment, and attitudes toward money and then report the results as news. The anchor announces, "Ninety-three percent of investors think investing in stocks stinks!" because after the closing bell at the end of a disappointing day reporters stuck microphones in front of disgruntled investors. Without poll results for filler, some station programming would be as full of holes as Swiss cheese.

As I've pointed out, how you ask a question can determine the answer. If, in difficult times, you ask people if they think the country is lagging behind China in terms of growth today, many will say yes, which might indicate a lack of confidence in the United States; but if you polled them about whether they would like the United States to emulate Chinese economic policies, you'd get a very different picture. Pollsters may word their questions to get the responses they're hoping for.

Don't Equate the Volume of Coverage with the Importance of the Story

Though there were only a very few cases of swine flu in early 2009, the media covered every new incident relentlessly all spring long.

By the time the World Health Organization declared swine flu a pandemic in early June—in other words, when the disease had really developed into an actual threat—the story was barely noted by reporters and broadcasters. They were already covering the latest celebrity breakup, meltdown, or death.

On the other hand, as I've pointed out in the case of Madoff, news that barely makes it onto the radar may ultimately have a seismic impact.

Don't Fall for the Numbers Game

The media like to use big round numbers to kick off a news cycle. I've mentioned the widespread glee when the Dow first hit 10,000 in 1999. The extensive media coverage went on for weeks. And when it retreated from a high of 14,000 to 10,000 in 2008, the handwringing in the press began, more frantic with each subsequent decline, to 9,000, 8,000, and so on. When it rebounded to 10,000 in October 2009, the positive headlines started anew.

Pundits are brought in to opine about these "milestones" as if they have some particular significance. They don't.

Do Look for Context

All-news radio spends a day promoting the fact that new statistics for employment or manufacturing or whatever will be coming out the next morning. But those first numbers are just estimates. They're all subject to revision some 30 to 90 days later, and the final figures may differ significantly from the first ones. So it's foolish to start trying to manage your finances based on the early numbers, which are almost certain to be inaccurate.

And it's always important to put things in context. When you hear that unemployment has gone up to 9 percent, remember to calculate that also means that 91 percent of people *are* employed.

Recognize Volatility for What It Is

Volatility gives the press and broadcasters material for the news of the day, but for an investor, volatility is just a distraction and a detriment to your long-term financial well-being. Your goal is not to rush in to take advantage of the ups and to run away on the downs but rather to produce a steady, long-term source of income from your nest egg.

Business news coverage has taken its cue from sports coverage. Sportscasters love to analyze Babe Ruth's swing and Derek Jeter's fielding ability, to review performance stats and outcomes, to recall that Wade Boggs ate chicken before every game, and to recirculate the notion that stepping on the baseline puts a jinx on a pitcher. In a similar fashion, the financial media love to find arcane factoids or irrelevant trivia and read meaning into them.

The media also oversimplify results: If a company is increasing market share, it's the winner, and the company that's losing share is the loser. But the press may have failed to note that the management of the "losing" company made a strategic decision to take a new direction and focus on a different market with better future prospects.

The hockey player Wayne Gretzky once explained his success by saying that he didn't skate to the puck but rather to where the puck was going. The company that is currently losing share may be going just where it plans to be in the future, but the media may have missed the story.

Media coverage of minute-by-minute reporting is useful only to a trader—someone who capitalizes on short-term trends, inefficiencies, and the news of the day and makes money if a stock goes up or down a point or two.

Before the general public was online, there was a popular day-trading strategy based solely on the broadcasts of Dan Dorfman. A financial analyst and *Money* columnist, he was a "stock picker" for CNBC who went on the air at 2:10 ET daily. Whatever stock he recommended would immediately rise. Since at the time, only traders had instant access to transactions, they could buy what he recommended, then sell to the "outsiders" who were just getting their orders in.

At one point, the Chicago Board of Options Exchange instituted a "Dorfman Rule" that allowed its authorities to stop trading the options on a stock that Dorfman referred to on his show. (Sometimes the boost was so fast and so short-lived that in order to take advantage of it, you had to have bought and then sold by the time the commercial came on.)

The media is always reporting on trends that have happened or that they anticipate will happen in the near future. To a long-term investor, such movements are largely irrelevant. To protect your nest egg, you have to be planning for what will happen in the next 10 or 20 years.

Take Your Bathroom Break When the CEO Comes On

Remember, as I've mentioned, company spokespersons always have an agenda. They're either making excuses for what went wrong in the past or painting a very optimistic view of the future. So they're not an unbiased source of information. Keep that in mind when you listen to what they say.

What's more, as I'll explain, concentrating on developments at individual companies is not the most effective use of your time.

Judging Trustworthiness

It's hard to find reliable experts. Back in 1966, economist Paul Samuelson said that "Wall Street indexes predicted nine out of the last five recessions." Substitute "pundits" for "indexes" and the same holds true. There are permabears who have been saying the market will be crushed year after year and permabulls who say the opposite. Like a broken clock, which shows the right time twice a day, an expert who gets interviewed often enough will at some point be right.

Any analyst who gets enough press for a correct early call about which way the market's heading becomes the Wizard of Wall Street until he or she fails to predict a second major move. Then the press finds another go-to person. If you're thinking of selecting someone as your guru, first find out how long that person's been delivering the current message and what his or her track record has been.

Research ratings on stocks and bonds from brokerage firms have long been considered reliable. But in the past few years, it became clear that there was a clandestine relationship between brokerage firms and the large companies for whom they provided investment-banking services. Knowing that a negative report might mean the loss of a corporate client, the firms might have been inclined to temper any criticism.

The Internet is a great source of information, but much of it—even if unbiased—is benchmarked to items that may not be relevant to your situation.

If you're really going to go it alone and manage a substantial sum, I recommend that you buy a subscription from one of the major providers of independent investment research to investors—Morningstar, ValueLine, or Standard & Poor's. Yes, they are costly, but consider the cost in relation to your retirement portfolio, and you may decide it's money well spent.

The information you'll get is unbiased. In the first place, these firms are not compensated by the companies they cover, and in the second, they apply exactly the same criteria to analyze every company. They use a template with a quarterly or annual analysis of specific data points, and their editorial comment is clearly marked as analysts' ratings. While a fund might get a five-star rating from Morningstar, it might not be a five-star choice for you. Doing the research will help you decide whether it is.

Do Your Own Investigating

When people ask me how to find investments, I tell them not to rely on sources that are easily available. Since most of the information you get comes from someone with an agenda, you're better off going out to get it rather than waiting for it to come to you. There is inspiration everywhere.

Recently I was in Walmart, looking around to test my theory that the most expensive appliances were the ones made in the United States. When I examined the packaging, I realized that nowadays U.S.-made appliances were almost nonexistent. Virtually all appliances are made in China. From that kind of insight, you can get investment inspiration. You might begin to wonder if you should find more international investments.

Go online and start asking questions. That in turn may lead you to look at international mutual funds and ultimately to research the pitfalls and pluses of international investing.

A long time ago, Warren Buffett said to buy what you know. The more extensive your knowledge, the more of an edge you'll have. For example, I heard a speaker comment, very perceptively, "If someone doesn't have a passport, he's probably not thinking about investing internationally."

Listen for the Message

As I've said, what's off the radar may be the most important news. Despite the number of publications and broadcasters tracking Wall Street and the flood of information and conversation on the Internet, virtually no one predicted the biggest story of the decade: the great collapse of 2008. While the situation was heading for disaster, no one had reported what was going on with complicated and extremely risky products cobbled from subprime mortgages.

Tim Ryan, chief executive of the Securities Industry and Financial Markets Association (SIFMA), issued a mea culpa and said Wall Street had to accept the blame for the financial crisis when he testified before the U.S. Senate Committee on Banking, Housing and Urban Affairs in March 2009. But to my mind, some of the blame also had to go to the media, which gave Wall Street firms a great platform to trumpet its products because the firms were their advertising clients.

In the end, though, your focus should not be on where to place the blame but on how to protect your nest egg. You're the one in charge of whether it shrinks or grows. The more you listen and read, the more you'll know, the greater the number of possibilities you'll see, and the better you'll know which to choose and when to step on the brakes or the gas.

You have to learn to filter out the noise. Because no matter what the media says, you get the last word.

Key Takeaways

■ **The media is not your financial advisor.** The goal of the editors of the business pages and the producers of business broadcasts is to increase the size of their audiences, not to provide you with guidelines for best managing *your* finances. Whatever information you get from these sources, recognize it for what it is: generic material that should be a starting point for thought, not serve as an instruction manual. Don't make investment decisions based on the news of the day.

■ **The Internet is a great source of information—and misinformation, too.** Thanks to Google and other search engines, "mouse potatoes" who sit at home with a finger on the clicker have access to a vast amount of research material—all of it totally unfiltered. Whether the source is unbiased or reputable is not always apparent. Much of the time you can't even know if the information is current, so you may be making a decision based on a trend from the past. Unless and until you can confirm the reliability of the source, be extremely careful about how you use what you find.

■ **Don't seek news exclusively from sources that confirm your beliefs.** Clicking the remote, spinning the dial, or leafing through the periodicals until you find information that validates your own opinion may be a great way to find reassurance, but using only these sources to gather news and opinions is a huge mistake. Though it's human nature to trust information that confirms our preconceived notions and ignore that which doesn't, that's an unreliable approach. Before you plan your strategy, listen to the other point of view. Sometimes it might be the right one.

■ **Today's news is just today's news.** The daily gyrations of the market give reporters something to talk about and the opportunity to inject some drama by handling the economic and corporate news like sporting events. But don't get distracted by the focus on short-term events. What you need are insights into long-term trends that really affect your financial future.

■ **A serious investor has to invest in the right tools.** If you're investing on your own, get your information like professionals do—by subscribing to reliable reporting services such as Standard & Poor's or Morningstar. Not only will you get unbiased information, but you will get it in a standardized format that makes it easy for you to compare investment options.

5

Check the
Fine Print

AMERICANS ARE VERY SAVVY CONSUMERS. Offered an abundance of choices in many categories—117 brands of domestic beer, produced by 38 breweries; 120 lines of lipstick, manufactured by 57 European, Asian, and U.S. companies—we do our homework, weigh the possibilities, and choose the option that's right for us.

But when it comes to shopping for investments, it's another story. Clearly, the most important purchases you make are the ones you put in your portfolio. After all, you're relying on them to fund all your future purchases. So it's almost incomprehensible that financial consumers typically take so few pains to ensure that they are doing the right thing. In the recent financial debacle, Wall Street let its clients down, but Wall Street doesn't deserve all the blame. Their clients were partners in the dysfunctional dance.

Here's an analogy. Say you're shopping for a car. When you walk onto the lot, you understand the situation. You're there to look at a specific brand of product (a Chevrolet, perhaps), manufactured by a parent company (General Motors, in this case), and sold by arrangement through a local distributor. You don't expect the salespeople to talk about Toyotas or Hondas or to bring up the fact that one of

79

them—or any other brand—might do better than Chevrolets on fuel consumption, cause less environmental impact, or boast a better safety record.

As a matter of routine, we check around if we're buying a car. Before or after we get onto that lot, we'll read magazine reviews of the car, go online, or talk to other people to check whether some other brand has a model that better suits our needs and concerns. What's more, when car salespeople tell us about the features and benefits of a product, we listen to their advice but factor in the knowledge that we have gleaned from our homework. We know their presentations are designed to highlight the features of the vehicles that their company is offering, which are indeed suitable to meet our transportation needs.

But they have no obligation to ensure that the particular brand they represent is the one best suited to our particular situation. The salespeople know—and we know—that making that judgment is our responsibility.

People are far less diligent when they shop for financial products. Many investors are clients of what I call the BIGCOs, the financial organizations with brand names. Sometimes, though, I think the clients forget that these BIGCOs are businesses. They not only create financial products, but they also back the products up with enormous marketing and advertising budgets; and they hire salespeople, who are called registered representatives. What many people fail to recognize is that these representatives wear two hats. One is to present the products offered by their firms, and the other is to advise us as to which of those best suits our needs.

Like the car dealers, brokers are required to sell you a suitable solution; they're permitted by law to sell you their solution only; and they have no legal obligation to sell you the best solution that is available anywhere. Just as you don't expect the Chevy dealer to tell you that you may find something better elsewhere, you can't expect a BIGCO to offer income-producing or growth-producing investments that may be more appropriate for you but are only available from a competitor.

In the financial debacle of 2008, a huge percentage of the money lost by back-porch America—that is, individual investors—was lost by the clients of the largest brokerage firms. That's because most people never truly knew whether they had the most appropriate holdings in their portfolios and if all the pieces fit together. Many began to question whether the products they had bought at the "dealership" where they parked their money were the best ones for their particular situation.

The brokers didn't foist the products on their clients. They just presented their offerings, often in response to a specific request. They might deliver what you're asking for, but you may not fully recognize the tradeoffs that come with the request you're making. If you're asking for an investment that produces a high rate of return, you have to be prepared for the inherent risks that investment carries.

The Least You Need to Know

You need to know what you're buying. As a client, you need to understand the long-term consequences of your investments. You have to ask the questions.

What's the basic business proposition I'm buying into when I make this investment? Ask what milestones the venture needs to achieve so you know it's on track to get the desired results; ask what could affect its ability to do so; and determine what early signs would indicate that it's failing.

What's the risk? A basic rule of investing says that the bigger the return, the bigger the risk. If safe investments are producing 3 percent, and you're offered a product in the same category that's returning 7 percent, that doesn't necessarily mean the product is bad. For example, a bond from a startup company may pay a high rate of return because it's a fledgling with uncertain prospects; but people may be willing to take the risk because they are looking for an extra return. But you should understand what kind of risk you're taking. If any investment is presented as "very safe" but is paying an unusually high return, ask your broker why.

What are the costs? The cover of every prospectus indicates the basic terms of the deal and the fee or commission the seller will earn. But the real costs can add up to far more than that. Look through the prospectus for the management fees, the transaction fees, and the fees paid to record keepers. Conflicts of interest may create other, not-so-obvious fees. For example, if you're buying a bond fund, the bond-trading desk of the company might be selling bonds to the fund and charging the fund a markup on those bonds.

The total of all the fees involved may come to three times what you expected. So that means the investment needs to make significantly more than your initial expectations in order to be an economically viable proposition for you.

And by the way, if you don't feel qualified to decipher exactly what's going on, ask your broker to give you a synopsis of all the internal and administrative fees.

How easy is it to get out? Some of the documents take two or three pages to explain what formula they use to price the investment and how frequently the pricing takes place. The pricing and its frequency affect your ability to take your money out. In some cases, you may have to wait 60 or 90 days. Even though you may be buying this investment for the long term, ask your broker what procedures would be involved should you have to sell it prior to the maturity date.

The Answer You Never Want to Hear

The red flag should go up if, in response to any of your requests, your broker says, "Let me get Bob, our product specialist, on the line." That is a very clear signal that your broker is showing you a product that is so complicated even he or she doesn't understand its true risks and benefits.

To understand how this situation came about, you have to go back to May 1, 1975, often referred to as May Day in the financial industry. On that date, the system of minimum fixed commission rates on stock sales—a system that had been in place since 1792—was abolished. Before May Day, only brokers could trade securities.

$8,500-a-month obligation or that there would be a staggeringly large balloon payment due within a couple of years. The borrowers, who got the lower payments that they asked for, didn't spend time reading the fine print.

In the same way, clients who observed that the stock market was booming went to stockbrokers because they wanted to be in on the action. Those brokers, too, responded to their clients' requests by putting together a portfolio without helping the clients make long-term calculations.

Both sets of brokers provided solutions, but not the best solutions for their clients. For example, an interest-only loan is appropriate for borrowers who have an irregular income stream. It gives them the flexibility to make modest payments in some months but assumes they will make correspondingly higher payments in the course of a year so the mortgage gets paid down in a timely fashion. Borrowers are even given a schedule of suggested payments to get the desired result. But for borrowers who routinely paid only the smaller amount, the mortgage became toxic.

Similarly, investors could be misled about the appropriateness of their investment. A bond paying an unusually high rate of interest, issued by a company whose prospects are iffy, might make sense for investors who understand that they're taking stock-like risks in exchange for a high return and who adjust the rest of their portfolios accordingly. But it would be a bad choice for investors who would be tempted by the yield and not recognize that they are taking on such risk.

How'd We Get Here?

In the pre-2008 years, in response to investors eager to get into the rising market, Wall Street came up with newer, more complicated products. Some of them promised both safety and high returns, two goals that had always seemed incompatible and contradictory.

Everyone was drinking the Kool-Aid, it seemed. As products became more and more complicated, and, as I have pointed out, fewer and fewer people understood them, investors and Wall Street professionals alike were holding their collective breath, trusting that what they were buying would actually accomplish the desired outcome.

Very few people fully grasped the risks of the business propositions the prospectuses outlined. This is typically the case, and not simply because the prospectuses are complex. A prospectus gives little insight into the likelihood of the company's (or offering's) success but describes in great detail all the possibilities that something might go wrong. Prospectuses are so generally negative that people no longer pay attention to the warnings, like the city dwellers who don't react when car alarms go off. Prospectuses really don't offer substantive insight into the likelihood that the venture will succeed. Their primary purpose seems to be to preclude lawsuits by investors who claimed they weren't sufficiently warned of the risks in the event the venture fails.

Whether people didn't understand the warnings or simply chose to ignore them, in 2008, everyone's report card came home. Trust was lost. When your investments blew up and the people who sold them to you couldn't explain why, your faith in their ability to make the best decisions for you was shaken.

Many of the executives and employees of BIGCOs were among the biggest losers, because they themselves had invested in the products they were selling. The catastrophe not only affected the brokers' pocketbooks along with their clients', but also, and perhaps more significantly, it shook the brokers' faith.

There was a mass exodus out of the big firms by brokers who felt they'd been duped. They had taken the word of their research people and quoted it to their customers. A broker who had 100 clients in an investment that didn't deliver as promised felt 100 times as betrayed as any one of his clients, for he had made a representation that money was safe in these investments 100 times over.

While everyone wanted someone to blame, you don't see headlines screaming about Bernie Madoff-type lawsuits being filed against BIGCOs. That's because at the core, they were complying with all relevant laws.

That was the great revelation to the investing public post-2008. Oh, sure, there was a public outcry: Where had the regulators been? Had the Securities and Exchange Commission (the SEC) been asleep at the wheel? In fact, not only had securities laws been in place, but also they had worked as originally intended.

When you prepare an investment offering, the SEC asks a million questions: *Who is in charge? Who stands to gain? What are the management fees, the commissions, the potential conflicts of interests, and the risk factors?* The questions are intended to make certain the facts are out in the open and the prospective buyer knows if the fees are huge, the commissions excessive, and the risk factors daunting. The SEC does not require an analysis of the likelihood that the desired outcome will be achieved. Its concerns are disclosure, not efficacy.

The outrage is that so much wealth was destroyed while, for the most part, the letter of the law was followed. The Securities Exchange Act, passed in 1934, obliges broker/dealers to present their clients with a basic description of the business proposition plus the risk factors and potential conflicts of interest between the buyer and seller.

Broker/dealers are required only to present investments that are "suitable" to their clients' needs. They are not obligated to put their clients' needs (to meet long-term goals) before their own (to make short-term profits).

This lack of imperative is what led to the birth of the independent investment advisory industry. The Investment Adviser Act of 1940 was enacted to establish a higher standard: "fiduciary" (from the Latin word for "faith" or "trust") responsibility. This means an obligation for advisors to act always in the client's best interest.

It is not illegal for a broker to suggest an investment that's suitable rather than one that would be better—motivated, perhaps, because the former pays the broker a higher commission. By contrast, a financial advisor, who receives a fee for services, would be acting illegally if he or she did not put your interests before their own.

Over the years, though, the general public never really understood that the level of responsibility for stockbrokers and registered investment advisors was not the same—that advice from a broker had only to meet a suitability standard while advisors were held to a fiduciary standard. Although the law was very clear on this point, consumers were not. That became ultra-evident subsequent to the market meltdown of 2008, when so many people realized that they were holding investments that were not exactly right for them.

Not surprisingly, one of the cornerstones of the financial regulatory reforms that President Obama signed into law in July 2010 is a mandate that the Securities and Exchange Commission (SEC) resolve the confusion. The intent would be to ensure that any financial professional offering advice to the public would always put a client's interests first.

Regardless of what the government and financial industry do, you have the ultimate fiduciary responsibility to yourself and the people who are depending on you. Yet a lot of investors spend much more time thinking about what car to buy than about putting together a portfolio. *Caveat emptor*. Let the buyer beware.

The Fault Might Be Yours

Since a Michigan dentist made the first online trade on July 11, 1983, many investors have taken the do-it-yourself (DIY) route. Online trading really gained traction after AmeriTrade introduced "Accutrade for Windows" in January 1996. Many people started with a thousand dollars or so, and once they became comfortable with the process, they began to run their own portfolios. The notion of caveat emptor applies to them as well.

Online traders, like BIGCO clients, may fail to read or understand what they are buying. And, like BIGCO clients, DIY investors may fall into the trap of the one-stop-shopping method of portfolio construction—most typically when they divide all their holdings among a single family of mutual funds.

Though this is diversification, it is not the right way to go about it. The product line of a single organization is unlikely to provide the best solutions to each of your particular needs.

Another retail analogy: Each counter in the cosmetics department of large department stores features a different brand, and the clerks at the counter represent that brand exclusively. So if you walk up to the L'Oréal counter and say you want a moisturizing skin cream that also fights the effects of aging, and a mascara that is hypoallergenic and builds volume, the clerk will sell you the L'Oréal products that best meet those criteria. If you happen to walk to the Clinique counter with the same request, you'll be shown Clinique's solutions. And so on.

At each counter, you will be offered an appropriate solution for your needs in each category and even an effective sales spiel, but you can't be sure that the best item at that counter is the best product in the store for your criteria. L'Oréal may have the preferred skin cream for you, but Clinique mascara may be your best choice.

There's a parallel to buying from a single family of funds. A particular family's large-cap or fixed income funds may be exceptional performers, while their small-cap and international funds might be worse than average. You might be better served by building a portfolio that's a mix of funds from several companies.

The Pitfalls of Online Trading

The computerized programs that the online trading companies pitch to investors managing their own portfolios would be laughable if they hadn't caused so many people to lose so much money.

They're taking a quant approach: using formulas to divine the optimum trade. Basically, they use patterns and templates of investments that have performed well in the past to track current markets to see if any of these patterns are being replicated. Then the programs alert you if they are. The notion is that if you buy what has worked in the past, you'll have a future winner. If only investing were as simple as that.

Perhaps the biggest pitfalls in do-it-yourself trading are the very factors that seem to be its greatest advantages. One is the ability to buy stock without paying big commissions. The other is ease and speed of use.

For one thing, I challenge the idea promoted in so many commercials that saving the costs of commissions is the path to wealth. The real effect of not having to pay commissions is that traders are encouraged to make possibly pointless, lateral moves just as you might take a longer alternative route rather than sit in traffic— merely to give yourself the sensation of motion. Very likely, the DIY traders wind up trading their own accounts more than any broker would have.

But it's not whether you save commissions or waste time that determines whether you'll be successful as an online trader. It's how well you can check your tendency to act on impulse—behavior that is facilitated by the Internet. Markets are open 24/7, and you can send your money around the world as fast as Scotty could beam Captain Kirk aboard the *Enterprise*.

The ads that invite you to open an e-trade account stress how fast and simple it is to use. But having powerful tools without having the skills to manipulate them just gives you the ability to mess things up in more elaborate ways.

Wait a week to make a decision? You're a dinosaur. Once you have information, there's pressure to move on it. But the chance of making a good decision is probably in inverse proportion to the speed at which it's made.

Note that in the Ameritrade ads—the ones that suggest that trading is simple enough for even a baby—the baby throws up right after he places an order. It's remarkably simple to turn a flicker of an idea into a $10,000 decision and, potentially, into a $10,000 mistake.

But the biggest detriment to the long-term financial health of the DIYer, I feel, is that when things don't go as expected, they don't have a professional to help them reevaluate and rethink their decisions.

Of course as a professional advisor my view is biased; but the fact is that you don't go it alone in most other important areas—from renovating your house to maintaining your health to analyzing your insurance coverage. Why on earth should your finances, which sustain every other aspect of your life, be the one area where you don't reach out?

Tricks of the Trade

To lure investors, promoters often resort to obviously manipulative tactics:

■ *Creating a false sense of urgency.* This approach is most commonly used to pump up the profile of a small company about which little information is available. Insiders somehow start a buzz suggesting that some event or announcement will take place that will dramatically affect the price of a stock. The insiders' goals are to drive up the price of the stock, unload it, and leave the newcomers holding the bag.

■ *Promising huge returns from minute investments.* You've most likely heard this pitch in the infomercials where a spokesperson tells you how a small real estate investment reaped a bonanza. Even given that the spokesperson is a real person and not an actor, his story may not be typical. Today there are plenty of "For Sale" signs around and fewer real estate come-ons. Where these schemes fall short is that the promoters are generally attentive during the courtship. But once seduced, you're pretty much on your own to make the deal pay off.

■ *Offering immediate results.* This is likely a tip-off that the deal is a Ponzi scheme, where the way that money is made is simply by roping in new people. The promoter uses the fresh dollars to pay off the existing investors, but when funds dry up, the last folks in are left holding the bag.

■ *Promoting questionable opportunities abroad.* Every would-be investor has heard about money to be made in developing countries. Now, thanks to the fact that businesses can be set up and run online without the inconvenience of phone calls, postage service, and complicated exchange rate transactions, Internet charlatans have been quick to take advantage. A victim of such a scheme has little recourse against someone who is outside the reach of the U.S. law enforcement agencies.

Most people don't fall for such obvious ploys. But they let their guard down when they believe the messenger to be credible.

The CNBC documentary "House of Cards" reported on people everywhere whose lives were turned upside down by the financial collapse, among them the mayor of a small Norwegian town. The town's budget was destroyed because she and the other city leaders had invested in U.S. mortgage derivatives that went sour.

The mayor said she had learned two things from her experience.

First, "If something looks too good to be true, it is." All the great financial frauds in history have been pulled off by people who appealed to the greed of investors in ways that in hindsight looked preposterous. That's because if we want to believe something that seems implausible, our rationalizing skills kick in. We convince ourselves that there's an explanation that we simply don't understand.

That's especially true today, when the industry has gotten more and more technical and the products have become complicated way beyond the comprehension of anyone who isn't a college-level mathematician. So the simple rule is: Don't buy something you don't understand. It's a bad move; and, besides, it's unnecessary.

Also, said the mayor, "I have learned not to trust nice men in Armani suits."

The clients of Bernie Madoff and other con artists got burned when they left everything in the control of others. The reality is that you must be an active participant in guarding what's important to you.

Act in Your Own Interest

In the final analysis, investors were badly hurt in the 2008 meltdown not for the reasons they thought. It wasn't that the SEC wasn't regulating things properly or that armies of Bernie Madoffs were stealing their money. It wasn't that market pundits misled them or that mortgage brokers gave them bad advice.

Perhaps it's because people asked for what they wanted—for example, stability with a high rate of return—without asking enough questions to understand that you can't have both simultaneously.

In order to reclaim your nest egg, you have to act in your own fiduciary interest. You have to take control, you have to develop a plan and your own set of principles, and you have to have conviction that what you're doing is right.

Key Takeaways

- **Know what you're buying.** Prospectuses are written by lawyers and read as if they're written for other lawyers, so investors tend to ignore them—at their own peril. You have to understand what you're buying: what fees are involved, what risks you're taking, what is the nature of the investment, and what are the rules and costs of exiting. Certainly the person who's selling it to you should be able to explain those details. Ask questions, and if the answers aren't clear, keep your money in your pocket.
- **Know how what you're buying fits into your portfolio mix.** You need to know that a prospective investment complements your other holdings—that it doesn't duplicate what you already have or that it will indeed play a necessary role in your portfolio. If you're working with an advisor, ask the purpose of a recommended purchase in terms of your overall investments. This will not only help you decide whether the investment is appropriate for you, but it will also cause you to review the overall composition of your portfolio.
- **Make sure your advisor is putting your interests first.** If you rely on someone to vet your investment choices, it's critical that the ideas that person is bringing to you are only those that will best serve your needs. The distinction between what is suitable for your needs and what is in your fiduciary interest is a significant one. Ask your advisor to agree to meet a fiduciary standard when making recommendations.
- **Don't be swayed by a brand name.** People who bought into the advertising pitch that the quality of advice from a nationally known brokerage firm would be superior learned that it was not necessarily so. Similarly, you can't assume that a big-name family of funds offers the best performers in every category.
- **There are no shortcuts to investment success.** You can't rely on guidance from a computer program that uses historical pattern-matching to send you alerts telling you that it's time to act. Automated solutions just produce information overload and promote a lot of pointless lateral moves. They can rob your financial future because they're simply focused on finding you the hot trade of the day.

6

Embrace a
Game Plan

IS YOUR PORTFOLIO PLANNED, or is it a random collection of acquisitions? If you're typical, it's probably a hodgepodge that includes blue chips and impulse buys, stocks you've held onto because they've performed well and others you've held because you hope they recover, some bought on the recommendation of a friend who claimed to "know something" and others bought on the advice of a broker who you hope knows something.

Here's a test of your faith in the securities you're holding: Which of them would you be willing to recommend to someone else? You're unlikely to have significant knowledge about every one of the 20, 50, or even more companies you've invested in. Probably you have only a vague idea about most. Realistically, it's impossible to have conviction about the prospects of each of dozens of companies.

That's what leaves you so vulnerable when times get rocky. If a particular investment goes south and you discover what about it you failed to analyze, you begin to wonder what stones you failed to turn over regarding your other holdings. Losing faith in one area shakes your confidence about the other decisions you've made—and your certainties collapse like dominos.

That loss of conviction—in combination with the head trash you're carrying, the current noise from the media, and uncertainty about the wisdom of your investment decisions—can leave you directionless and anxious.

Since it's clearly impossible to have conviction about every single investment position, your solution is to have conviction in your overall investment strategy. And that leaves you with what I believe is the most prudent, reliable, and inevitable choice: asset allocation, the investment philosophy based on diversification. The folk wisdom of Yogi Berra sums it up very simply:

When you come to the fork in the road, take it.

Get above Tree Level

Most investors are confused because they're down on the ground making their investment decisions, choosing among the leaves. But once you get above tree level, you realize that investing is not as complicated as it may seem. Every kind of investment finds its origin in just one of five categories—currency, equities (stocks), debt (bonds), real estate, and commodities (food products, fuel, and minerals). Everything else is just an offshoot of these five.

Dividing your money among several categories can achieve all the desired goals: reduce risk, produce income, and offer the potential for growth.

Exactly how you make the allocations depends on a number of factors, including your appetite for risk, age, income, tax bracket, time horizon, and objectives. But no matter what specific choices you make, proper asset allocation will increase your ability to sleep at night.

The reason it works is very basic: Different categories of investments have different rates of return and volatility. The very conditions that depress the price on certain investments may boost it on others. For example, when the stock market is rising, bond prices generally go down, and vice versa.

But asset allocation is not just a way to reduce risk and provide income, which are only two of your three goals. Many people are surprised to learn that asset allocation is also the best way to improve your chances of a strong return.

According to modern portfolio theory, developed by economist Harry M. Markowitz—who won the Nobel Prize for his work—of the factors that determine the overall outcome of your portfolio, an astounding 91.5 percent of that outcome is due to asset allocation. Market timing contributes under 2 percent and individual securities selection, under 5 percent.

Though it seems sensible to focus on the area that has more than 90 percent of the impact on your nest egg rather than the areas that combined make up less than 10 percent, most people do the opposite.

Asset Allocation and the Style Quilt

To explore the idea of asset allocation, you have to become familiar with the "style quilt." Financial professionals use the quilt as a graphic illustration in support of this approach. The style quilt has horizontal and vertical squares, each representing a different kind of investment. Horizontally, the quilt is arranged by years, with the most recent positioned the furthest to the right. Vertically, it's organized by asset category; the top performer in the quilt is on the top of the column, the lowest on the bottom.

A style quilt can be constructed in many ways. The squares (called style boxes) can represent a mixture of all the five asset categories. Or the quilt may be used to illustrate what's going on in only one or two categories. For example, a style quilt comprised only of equities (stocks) may include style boxes that represent different sectors, such as health care, technology, and financials. A style quilt comprised of a mixture of stocks and bonds may include style boxes for taxable and tax-free bonds as well as boxes representing stocks of small, medium, large, and mega-large companies.

But every style quilt makes the same point: that no individual type of investment is a sure bet. In every quilt, the individual squares move around in an utterly random fashion—some years at or near the top, some at or near the bottom.

Human beings are comfortable with patterns. We try to find them even when they don't exist. With investments, the only pattern is that there is no pattern.

Take a look at the style quilt in Figure 6.1. This quilt has style boxes representing all five basic categories, and, in the case of stocks and bonds, subsets of the category. After 9/11/01, note that cash and bonds (which are generally perceived as the most conservative investments) were the best-performing categories; but as world events settled down, they were weaker performers.

In 2008, when everyone again ran for safety during the economic crises, cash and bonds were again the place to be. But when the market heated up in 2009, the pendulum swung again, and they were out of favor. The up and down movement of the boxes is more a reflection of current events and sentiment than any other factor.

Look specifically at the Mega Cap—Dow Jones boxes (black boxes), which represent the largest of the large companies in the

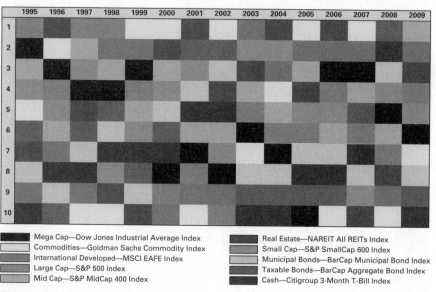

Figure 6.1 Asset Class Quilt

Source: Mercadien Asset Management.

United States. You'll see the relative performance of the Dow has bounced around quite a bit over the 15-year period. In 1995 it was nearly the top-performing sector, but 10 years later in 2005 it was the worst. While the Dow is only one choice in a style quilt, what happens to the Dow has a disproportionate effect on the collective psyche.

The Dow and "The Market"

When people gather around the water cooler or the table and talk about how well or poorly the market is doing, and when the media reports on the ups and downs of the market, both groups are usually referring to the Dow Jones Industrial Average (DJIA, or simply "the Dow"). It represents not simply a single asset category—stocks—but also a subset of that category. The stocks that make up the Dow are exclusively the largest U.S. companies, worth at least $200 billion apiece, and the Dow includes only 30 of them.

Because it tracks only huge companies and just a limited number of them, the Dow is not nearly as accurate a barometer of U.S. business as the S&P 500, which tracks 500 companies of varying sizes. Nevertheless, most investors and the media use the Dow as an overall indicator, to analyze past and current trends, and even to predict where the market is headed in the future. And the rise and fall of the Dow determines their collective psychological mood.

The Dow has always had ups and downs, perhaps none so dizzying as in the last decade. So when people say to me, "I want to get out of the market," what they're really saying is that they don't like the volatility of the 30 stocks represented on the Dow. Based on its irregular, stomach-churning performance, I wouldn't want all my money there, either.

In the show *The Search for Signs of Intelligent Life in the Universe*, comedian Lily Tomlin defines reality as "nothing more than a collective hunch." The same could be said of the Dow. The companies indexed on the Dow are chosen by a committee of editors of the *Wall Street Journal*, and collectively the companies are meant to represent a good mix of industries. There are no fixed rules that determine how the Dow stocks are selected, and the list doesn't even include all the largest companies in the country.

What's more, the list changes. It's periodically "reconstituted" to include companies that are more reflective of the times. On June 1, 1959, the year in which the last of the baby boomers were born, the reconstituted list looked like this:

Allied Chemical	General Electric Company	Sears Roebuck & Company
Aluminum Company of America	General Foods	Standard Oil of California
American Can	General Motors Corporation	Standard Oil (NJ)
American Telephone & Telegraph	Goodyear	Swift & Company
American Tobacco B	International Harvester	Texaco Incorporated
Anaconda Copper	International Nickel	Union Carbide
Bethlehem Steel	International Paper Company	United Aircraft
Chrysler	Johns-Manville	U.S. Steel
DuPont	Owens-Illinois Glass	Westinghouse Electric
Eastman Kodak Company	Procter & Gamble Company	Woolworth

Nearly 40 years later, on June 8, 2009, the list looked like this:

3M Company	DuPont	McDonald's Corporation
Alcoa Incorporated	ExxonMobil Corporation	Merck & Company, Incorporated
American Express Company	General Electric Company	Microsoft Corporation
AT&T Incorporated	Hewlett-Packard Company	Pfizer Incorporated
Bank of America Corporation	Home Depot Incorporated	Procter & Gamble Company
Boeing Corporation	Intel Corporation	Travelers Companies
Caterpillar Incorporated	International Business Machines	United Technologies
Chevron Corporation	Johnson & Johnson	Verizon Communications Inc.
Cisco Systems, Inc.	JPMorgan Chase & Company	Walmart Stores Incorporated
Coca-Cola Company	Kraft Foods Inc.	Walt Disney Company

In other words, when people talk about this thing called "the market," they aren't talking about one unchanging thing. Over the years, what constitutes a representative group of companies has changed significantly, and many individuals have spent many hours collectively trying to pick the right selection—and then revising it to keep it relevant to the current environment.

Look at all the work the professionals put into maintaining the relevancy of the Dow, and then consider how much work you'd have to do to keep your personal index current. Not only would you have to make certain the list accurately reflected the current environment, but also you would have to be sure its composition was relevant to your own particular situation.

Yet, despite the extraordinary amount of work involved in selecting just the right companies, keeping the list current, and then continually reevaluating the companies to make sure that they suit your ongoing needs, some people still believe that being a successful investor is a simple matter of picking and buying the right stocks. Many books on the personal finance shelves subscribe to this approach and offer various strategies to get the right shopping list.

If you have the time and inclination to study individual companies, there's no doubt that you acquire some useful knowledge. But if you're a typical investor, as I've explained, being a stock picker is a poor use of your time.

In any event, trying to create the shopping list, which was always hard, has become more confusing than ever now that there are so many investment choices. Years ago, for one thing, there were fewer companies trading publicly. Also, the international selection of investments was much smaller and the opportunities were much more limited. You couldn't trade real estate and commodities like stocks, as you can today. And doing research was extremely difficult. A lot of data back then was available only through a broker.

Today there are many more choices to consider, both here and abroad. And, thanks to the Internet, there's a staggering volume of easily accessible information. Even with computers, it's hard to imagine a single investor having the inclination or the stamina to sift through it all. Those are more reasons to adopt asset allocation as a philosophy.

Each Category Plays a Role

Asset allocation gives you the best of all worlds. In the event of a broad downturn, you're positioned to smooth out the highs and the lows, and if things are going well you're going to be in on the party.

Ultimately you'll have to pick specific investments, but when your overall strategy is asset allocation, the specific holdings lose their individual significance. You should spend most of your time considering two things only: What asset categories do you need to be invested in, and how much do you need of each?

Most investors believe they have an either/or option: being in the market and taking risks, or playing it safe and sticking to bonds. That's like believing the only two food categories are shellfish or fruit. Not only are there other categories of investments, but also there are subcategories of stocks and bonds that expand the possibilities even further. To make the decision about what you want to hold, you need to understand what role each asset class plays.

Currency for Short-Term Needs

Currency (cash) is the one asset category where growth is irrelevant. You need cash to cover your short term-needs.

And you also hold some cash in reserve, as what I call "dry powder"—to access in case of emergency so you don't have to upset your overall plan by selling stock at a bad time or redeeming a high-yielding bond before it reaches maturity.

In the past I've recommended keeping a cash reserve large enough to pay your bills for six months, but in the aftermath of 2008 a lot of people have been revising that calculation upward. What's appropriate for you is a matter of your comfort level. Pick a number that allows you to sleep through the night. If you're still tossing and turning even when you have a six-month reserve, put aside enough for a year. The only downside to holding excessive cash is that it loses value to inflation.

Much of the media noise regarding currency has to do with the relative value of the currencies of different countries: what the yen is worth, say, compared to the dollar. A British pound, for example, might have been pegged at $1.45 and then risen in worth to $1.65, and you can treat that movement as if it were a stock investment. I don't recommend that the average investor get involved in currency trading. It's a specialty area best left to professional traders. Besides, the factors that affect currency are part of the movement of the stocks, bonds, and real estate of every country. If you're investing internationally, you're already involved in this asset class as a byproduct.

Bonds as a Source of Income

Bonds are generally used to provide a predictable income stream. For retirees, that income stream can replace a paycheck.

Usually issued in denominations of $1,000, bonds are actually loans made by investors to three types of borrowers: companies, which use the funds to finance new business projects; local and state governments, which use the money to build roads, bridges, sewers and schools and finance other public works; and the federal government, which uses the money to pay for things like national defense, operational costs, student loans, and infrastructure.

Every bond states the rate of interest, the amount you'll receive annually and the length of the term. It also spells out special conditions—for example, whether the bond is callable, which means that the borrower may pay it back before the end of the term. (That usually happens when interest rates fall. The borrower may want to pay off an outstanding debt in order to borrow at lower rates.) If a bond is not called, the borrower pays you the face value at the end of the term.

You can buy or sell bonds in a secondary market. Whether you'll pay more or get less than the face value (par) depends on the current interest rate. Bond buyers are looking for income, so bond prices move in the opposite direction from the yield.

If you bought a bond when rates were at 3 percent but today rates are up to 4 percent, a potential buyer will offer you less than $1,000. But if current rates are 4 percent and your bond is paying 5 percent, you can sell it for a premium. Such repricing is called mark to market—that is, the price is marked to return whatever the market is currently yielding.

Bonds are generally considered a reliable and conservative investment. A bond's value is determined by three criteria: how it's rated (which is based on the riskiness of the loan), its duration (the length of the loan), and whether the income is taxable.

Every investment involves risk. With bonds, the risk is that the issuer won't pay interest on time or, at the end of the term, won't return the principal. The creditworthiness of the issuer of a bond is determined by one of the ratings agencies.

Even though the agencies have been somewhat discredited—they facilitated the sale of bad mortgage loans by rating them too high—ratings are still the best available tool for a prospective buyer to judge the quality of a purchase.

The three top ratings agencies, Moody's, Standard & Poor's, and Fitch, all use a AAA rating to designate a top-rated bond and a D to indicate the lowest. Top ratings are usually given to bonds issued by the U.S. Treasury, highly rated municipalities, and companies with substance and a track record. The lower-rated bonds come from fledgling companies or companies that have fallen on hard times.

Since high-rated bonds present less repayment risk, they don't pay as high an interest rate as lower-rated ones. But you should choose safety over return with retirement funds, and invest them only in investment-grade bonds—bonds that are rated Baa or higher by Fitch, and BBB– or higher by the others.

Many small bonds are unrated for reasons unrelated to quality, but the lower-rated "high yield" bonds—also known as "junk bonds"—are likely to be too risky for an investor who is relying on them for retirement income.

The length of the term also affects the interest rate. The further away the payoff, the higher the rate, and some terms last for 30 years or more. The borrower pays more interest for the opportunity to tie up your money for longer periods, and the purchaser expects more interest because he's taking duration risk; that is, his money is unavailable for reinvestment into other opportunities.

When interest rates are low, long-term bonds aren't desirable. Since you'll have to wait a long time to get your money back, you'll probably want a higher rate of return than bonds customarily yield. But if rates are high, it might make sense to lock them in with a long-term bond.

Investment grade Treasury bills, federal agency bonds, corporate bonds, and mortgage-backed securities of various durations are taxable bonds—that is, the income you get from them is taxed as ordinary income.

Investment-grade municipal bonds of various durations pay lower rates, but you don't pay federal tax on the income; and if you buy bonds from your home state or city government, you don't pay those taxes, either.

Accounting considerations determine whether taxable or tax-free bonds are the appropriate choice for you.

Stocks for Growth

Bonds provide the certainty of daily bread but generally produce modest returns that make it difficult to keep pace with inflation. That's of special concern to retirees, because inflation usually has its greatest impact on the price of necessities such as food and fuel.

The impact of inflation is clearer if you consider it in dollar-and-cents terms. At a modest inflation rate of 3 percent, groceries that cost $100 this year will cost $134.39 10 years from now and $180.61 in 20 years.

Or, to look at it another way, 3 percent inflation reduces the purchasing power of $1,000 by almost half (to $543.79) in 20 years; at 4 percent it has the same effect in 15 years ($542.09), and at 5 percent, it does the same in 12 years ($540.36.)

I have warned against chasing high returns in retirement because of the associated risk, but you need some growth to ensure you'll still be able to afford bread—and the gas that will take you to the store to buy it. To cover the rising costs of maintaining your current lifestyle, you have to grow your money. Historically, the most reliable method of achieving long-term growth has been by investing in equities.

In buying shares, you're actually buying a piece of the company in hopes that it will prosper and your shares will ultimately be worth more than what you paid. Some stocks also produce modest income in the form of a dividend.

Stock prices fluctuate daily in accordance with the current perception—primarily the perception, not the reality—of a company's prospects. Since the stock price is subject to dramatic swings based on today's news, on a daily basis it's priced either too high or too low.

Even if over the long term a stock has been rising steadily, its short-term pattern is invariably a sawtooth pattern of ups and downs. So at the moment when you need to turn your investment into cash, it may be worth less than what you paid—or nothing at all. But if a company is a success, its stock can appreciate way beyond your expectations, and that of course is why stocks are alluring.

Stocks are generally described as small cap, mid cap, large cap, or—like the Dow companies—mega caps. *Cap* is short for capitalization, one measure of a company's size. The market capitalization of a company is calculated by multiplying the total number of shares outstanding by the current stock price.

Generally, a company is considered a mega cap if it has a market cap of $200 billion and up; big/large cap, $10 to $200 billion; mid cap, $2 to $10 billion; small cap, $300 million to $2 billion; micro cap, $50 million to $300 million; and nano cap, under $50 million.

Bear in mind that the market cap may not reflect the true value of a company as determined by its profits, its balance sheet, and its product position. In the dot.com bubble of the late 90s, the market caps of many companies that never made any money were huge; and a company that's doing well but not perceived as "hot" can have a low market cap.

Most investors want growth but find comfort in stability. That's why in general they prefer the mega caps represented by the Dow to a startup operating out of someone's garage or a company across the globe with an unpronounceable name. They understand what's going on when a Home Depot closes a store or a Macy's needs to run a sale to unload excess inventory. But those familiar companies represent only a relatively small range of the investment possibilities.

Real Estate Is Tangible

The great allure of real estate is its tangibility. As an investment class, real estate tends to move with the bond market because it is sensitive to interest rates. One of the reasons for the run-up in real estate prior to 2008 was that interest rates were so low that people found buying a house to be an affordable investment, and the increase in demand for ownership boosted prices. And since people didn't have to spend a lot of money to borrow money, they could allot more money toward the purchase price of the house.

Many people have made a significant real estate investment in their own homes, a fact they often fail to consider in making their asset allocation. If a conservative investor with a $1 million house has $1 million to invest and wants to put 50 percent into bonds, he should bear in mind that his real estate and bond investments together represent $1.5 million in two asset classes whose market values often react similarly. True, bonds serve a different purpose in a portfolio—they generate income—but the similarity should be taken into account for asset allocation purposes.

If you're interested in investing in real estate but don't have the cash required to purchase additional properties for rental income or for speculation, you can invest in real estate investment trusts (REITs), companies that sell shares like common stock. Buying REIT stock is like buying any stock, except that the company in this case is in the business of managing income-producing properties and distributes its profits as dividends.

Commodities: Investments in Economies

The style quilt in Figure 6.1 shows that commodities have especially dramatic swings. They're either at the top of the list or the very bottom.

Commodities are the products of the physical world: agricultural products and livestock, oil and gas, and precious metals and minerals. While you invest in stocks for the growth of a company, you invest in commodities for the growth of economies. Worldwide population growth means there is increased demand for commodities, so all categories are potentially good investments.

Commodities trade on supply and demand factors. Some classes of commodities are affected by the environment. Others are becoming more scarce—we have to dig deeper to find oil and mine more dirt to find copper—but new technology and new techniques are making it easier to access them.

Prices whipsaw, and it's hard to predict what's going to happen next. Such volatility isn't for the faint of heart.

International Investments: New Possibilities

Figure 6.2 shows the performance of stock markets here and in other countries. Note that although the United States (represented by the black boxes) was number two in 1995, it has ranked much lower since then.

While the United States at one time was the global growth powerhouse with no equal, today you have to pay a lot more attention to international investments. The expansion of technological expertise and the development of home-grown labor forces have helped level the playing field, enabling many other countries to become full players in the world market.

Now, a substantial amount of the world's growth—as measured by the cumulative gross domestic product (GDP) of each country—is driven by countries outside the United States, specifically those we consider emerging markets.

"Emerging markets," which are growing and volatile, include the BRIC countries (Brazil, Russia, India, and China) as well as many smaller nations. "Developed markets," in contrast, have more consistent GDPs, a more affluent and educated population, and a developed infrastructure; they are generally stable, self-sustaining, and self-correcting (i.e., they can take measures to keep inflation from spiraling out of control).

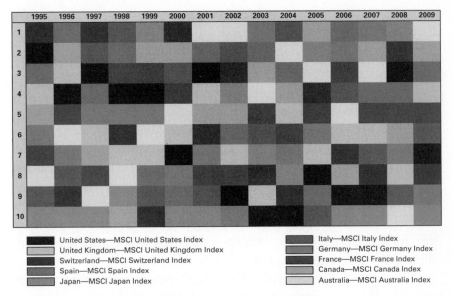

| | 1995 | 1996 | 1997 | 1998 | 1999 | 2000 | 2001 | 2002 | 2003 | 2004 | 2005 | 2006 | 2007 | 2008 | 2009 |

United States—MSCI United States Index
United Kingdom—MSCI United Kingdom Index
Switzerland—MSCI Switzerland Index
Spain—MSCI Spain Index
Japan—MSCI Japan Index

Italy—MSCI Italy Index
Germany—MSCI Germany Index
France—MSCI France Index
Canada—MSCI Canada Index
Australia—MSCI Australia Index

Figure 6.2 International Quilt (Developed Markets)

Source: Mercadien Asset Management. Data based on Morgan Stanley.

Since the goal of investors is to participate in growth, and an increasing amount of global growth is coming from emerging markets, it is shortsighted not to explore opportunities there as well as in other countries outside our borders.

But the real change in international investing is that it is no longer a simple matter of seeing what countries are prospering and finding investment opportunities in those places. The bigger take-away is that international investments are vital because economies around the globe are increasingly intertwined because of digital commerce.

Here's how the world works today: When you buy a blender manufactured in China at the local Walmart, a clerk scans the stock-keeping unit (SKU) number at the checkout and a computer reviews the inventory sheet. Recognizing that the blender is the last of a case of 12, it generates and sends a purchase order directly to China, where another computer selects another case of blenders at the factory and labels it in English for delivery to your local store. When the case arrives in the United States at Walmart's distribution center, it is routed like luggage, put on a truck, and delivered.

The procedures are highly organized, and they operate without communication barriers and virtually without human intervention.

Though the products, industries, and names differ, a similar scenario is repeated countless times every day around the globe. In a conversation I had with Fareed Zakaria, the *Newsweek* editor, *Washington Post* columnist, and CNN correspondent, he made the point that a GE aircraft engine is made of parts sourced from 22 countries, and the finished product is sold to customers in 16.

As scientists come up with new ways to expand bandwidth (the measure of how much information a network can transmit and how quickly) and sharing information becomes cheaper and cheaper, nations will become increasingly interdependent.

Consider that nearly half of the revenues that are generated by the companies represented in the S&P 500 (the largest companies in the United States) come from overseas. Then contemplate how many products you buy that aren't even manufactured here. Every county is both a producer and consumer of the goods and services of its neighbor.

Nearly 100 years ago, Calvin Coolidge said, "The business of America is business." His words are often cited to sum up the overconfidence in the U.S. economy that preceded the Great Depression. Investors today are in danger of making another miscalculation: investing with too strong a home-country bias.

Instead of seeing the opportunity elsewhere, we see a threat. There may be political risk in investing overseas, but as Zakaria has pointed out, we've seen in the past couple of years that there's also political risk investing exclusively in the United States. You have to recognize that places in the world are growing faster than we are, and no country is an island. Events that occur anywhere may have ramifications everywhere.

The Power of Stocks

The reason that financial professionals have a bias toward including stocks in most asset allocation plans is made clear in Figure 6.3,

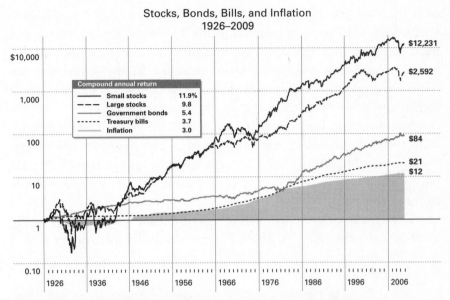

Figure 6.3 Stocks, Bonds, Bills, and Inflation, 1926–2009

Source: © 2010 Morningstar. All rights reserved. 3/1/2010.

Past performance is no guarantee of future results. Hypothetical value of $1 invested at the beginning of 1926. Assumes reinvestment of income and no transaction costs or taxes. This chart is for illustrative purposes only and not indicative of any investment. An investment cannot be made directly in an index.

known familiarly as the mountain chart, which compares the growth of various asset classes over more than eight decades.

As I've pointed out, the purchasing power of the dollar is eroded by inflation over time. Today you have to lay out $12 to buy what $1 bought back in 1926. To keep pace with inflation, your assets must grow as well.

The chart shows what $1 invested in 1926 would have grown to over time in each asset category. When you look, bear in mind that the final numbers don't reflect the bite that taxes would have taken out of your results.

Treasury bills, money lent to the Federal government, backed by its full faith and credit, are regarded by people everywhere as the safest possible investment—what I call "the world's mattress." Yet had you invested your $1 there it would have turned into just $21 before taxes over the past 84 years. By putting money in Treasuries, you'd have realized just a 3.7 percent return annually. This is an excellent example of what you give up in exchange for certainty. The "safest possible investment" would leave you in the worst position. Had you invested the $1 in government bonds, you would have gotten a 5.4 percent annual return and your $1 would have grown to a measly $84.

Not until you look at equity ownership do you see any meaningful return. If you had invested $1 in large cap stocks in 1926, your money would have grown 9.8 percent annually and your dollar would have turned into $2,592 by the end of 2009. That's a good example of money working for you.

The stocks of small companies have done even better, growing 11.9 percent annually. By 2009, your 1926 dollar investment would have become a whopping $12,231, making this sector the clear historical winner.

Still, I wouldn't make a case for investing exclusively in small cap stocks. Notice that as they go up, the lines get choppier: that is, volatility increases. If you'd been able to put your money in those small cap stocks and simply left it there, you'd have come out way ahead, but most people can't do that. There are times when you need to raise cash, and if any of those times had been when the volatile small cap market was in a slump, you'd have lost a lot of your assets.

You should now understand why it's worth your time and effort to maximize your return by even a very small amount. Over time, it can make a huge difference. Though the returns of large caps (9.8 percent) and small caps (11.9 percent) differed by only 2.1 percent, look at how compounding affected the total dollar amount: $1 in the former would have turned into $2,592 and in the latter, into $12,231.

Just as a small numerical difference can eventually translate into a huge difference in returns, a small tactical deviation can have tremendous consequences for your ultimate investment success. This is why establishing and sticking with core principles, the subject of the next chapter, is so critical.

Key Takeaways

- **Understand the role each investment plays.** Just as a carpenter carefully chooses which tool to pull out of his toolbox for every specific job, you too have to carefully choose from an array of investment "tools"—stocks, bonds, real estate, commodities, and cash—in putting together your portfolio. Each of them serves a different purpose and reacts differently to macro economic changes.
- **Diversify.** What makes one sector cold can make another hot, and you don't want to be stuck holding only the ziggers when it's the zaggers' turn. When you diversify, no single event will kill you: You avoid concentration risk, you smooth out volatility, and you get a better night's sleep.
- **Don't overcomplicate your allocation.** Think in terms of broad equities and debt classes rather than ABC company and XYZ bond. If you overcomplicate your asset allocation, you can get distracted by the minutiae. And when there are movements in the market, you won't understand how you're affected; instead of sticking with a plan, you may rethink your individual holdings with every shift and make unnecessary and ill-advised trades.
- **See opportunity, not danger, outside our borders**. Once upon a time, the United States was the only real global growth story, so it made sense to keep all your money here at home. Nowadays, you have only to look at the manufacturers' labels on the equipment in your office, your car, and your home to see the opportunities all around the globe. We're all very willing to use our purchasing dollars outside the United States; we have to get comfortable with deploying our investment dollars overseas as well.

7

Establish
Your Rules

IF ARCHITECT BONANNO PISANO had made it his goal to build an engineering marvel that would lure a steady stream of tourists for more than eight centuries, he couldn't have done a better job. But if his intention was to build a functional new bell tower for the cathedral of Pisa, he messed up big time.

A couple of years ago, I visited the Leaning Tower of Pisa, which was begun in 1173 A.D. It's a truly spectacular building, an example of Romanesque architecture that merges several styles to create what art historians have called a rare blend of vigor and serenity. But just five years after construction began, a major flaw became evident. The building was leaning to the side.

At the top, which is eight stories high, the tower is 12 feet out of plumb. It would have toppled over long ago without the wires that hold it in place. My guide explained that the problem is that the designer didn't do his homework. He broke ground on soil that was too soft.

I have warned you of miscalculating when you fail to think about the long term; being distracted by the trash in your head; being led astray by noise in the media; and being ill-informed about your financial decisions.

I have cautioned you to deal with that by selecting a strategy. Now I'm counseling you to develop principles.

To Reach a Goal, You Need a Plan

Most people don't have a good financial plan. Actually, many of them don't have a bad plan, either. Most of them, long experience has taught me, don't have any plan at all.

But they usually do have a goal. They want to maintain their accustomed lifestyle (or an even better one), they hope they don't run out of money before they've run out of heartbeats, and most of them would like to leave some sort of legacy. Unless you have tremendous resources, and sometimes even with them, you can't achieve that goal without a plan. Most people know that, but they don't do anything about it.

Just as a heart attack will drive someone to get serious about diet and exercise, a major economic change may spur people to start thinking about their finances. Knowing that, you'd think that the market upheaval of 2008 would have had such an effect. But you'd be wrong.

The Society of Actuaries published "A Supplemental Report on the Impact of the 2008–2009 Financial Crisis" in July of 2009. It reported on interviews that had been held in the spring of 2009, when the market had plunged dramatically.*

> [A year ago, in spring 2008] nearly three in 10 retirees had not estimated how many years their assets and investments *might* last in retirement and an additional one in 10 retirees had never thought about it. [In April 2009] a slightly larger proportion of retirees are reporting that they have not estimated this figure—34 percent have not estimated how long their assets and investments might last and 11 percent have not thought about it.

This means that in the spring of 2008, more than a third of retirees had never estimated how long their nest eggs would last. A year later, after they'd been subjected to an endless stream of

---

*Online at www.soa.org/files/pdf/news-pub-2009-difference.pdf.

devastating financial news, you'd think they'd finally have become motivated to plan for the future. Instead, the number of folks who remained clueless actually rose. The report comes to the only conclusion possible:

> The slight increase may be the result of retirees not wanting to face reality in light of the economic downturn.

There's a word for fear of planning: teleophobic. Teleophobes come up with all sorts of rationalizations. *I'm not comfortable with numbers. I don't know what questions to ask. I haven't found the right advisor.* But basically, they're just avoiding reality.

Having no plan can be a comfort, in a weird kind of way. You're lulled into a false sense of security. When you have nothing to measure your progress against, you're never falling behind. Without a specific destination, you never have to admit you're lost.

And having no plan actually creates a kind of default plan. You find immediate, short-term, Band-Aid solutions to money issues and tell yourself, *I've got deadlines at the office. I'm coaching the team. I have too much going on right now. I'll get around to it.* Or not.

Often it takes a catalytic event—the sale of a business, a divorce, or widowhood—to drive new clients to seek me out. Together, we construct a plan. And I explain that the plan works only if it's on a solid foundation.

You need a set of investment principles at the core at your decision-making. Some of the biggest mistakes investors make aren't related to their investment choices but are a result of ignoring the principles. As Bonanno Pisano learned, any softness at the core can topple what you've so carefully constructed.

Find the Right Balance

If the prospect of volatility kept you entirely out of stocks, or if the stress of volatility meant that you cashed out of your investments, you paid a heavy price. But tolerating some volatility can bring your portfolio a huge return.

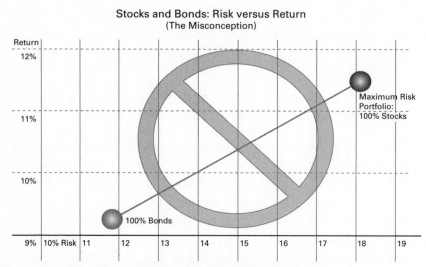

Figure 7.1 The Chart of Wrongheaded Thinking

New clients often tell me something like this: "I'm 70 years old, and I don't want any aggressive stuff in my portfolio. I just want to invest conservatively," and by conservative, they mean an all-bond portfolio. Their goal is to produce income.

In their mind's eye, such clients see Figure 7.1, or what I call the Chart of Wrongheaded Thinking: believing that adding more stocks adds more risk in an ever-climbing line. These people are giving up the returns on equity because they're not looking at the facts.

The man who pioneered the notion of asset allocation, Harry Markowitz, is also noteworthy for pointing out that adding some level of stocks to bonds actually makes a portfolio *more* "conservative." That's a huge aha moment for many investors.

To demonstrate, Markowitz came up with an idea that he called the Efficient Portfolio, which attempts to find the perfect balance between minimizing risk and maximizing gain. When you get the balance exactly right, you've reached what he called the Efficient Frontier. It's shown graphically in Figure 7.2. It demonstrates that during the years 1970 through 2009, the least volatile portfolio would have been

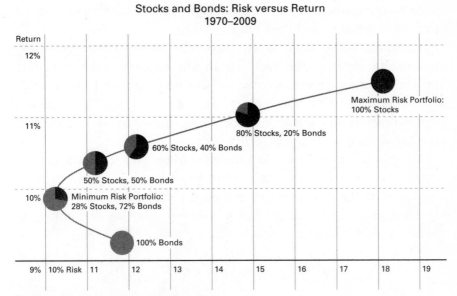

Figure 7.2 The Efficient Frontier

composed not of 100 percent bonds but of 72 percent bonds and 28 percent stocks.

The percentages don't stay constant because the relative performance of stocks to bonds changes annually. The lesson is that adding some equity exposure to a bond portfolio can decrease volatility and increase return. In fact, as the chart illustrates, historically you don't take on greater volatility until you get over 50 percent allocation to equities.

Meet Your Income Needs First

No retirement plan will be effective and enduring if it's not supported by a long-term income stream and cash reserves that together keep your reservoir full. When you start the decision-making process in asset allocation, the first thing you have to do is calculate the amount of cash you need to pay your bills.

Cash may come from current income or from income-producing investments. And, in the event of an interruption of your income flow (because you're unemployed or because your investments aren't generating income as expected), it has to come from what I referred to previously as dry powder: a reserve of funds you've put aside in very liquid short-term investments.

You want to avoid being in a situation where you're so strapped for cash that you have to sell securities to cover your immediate needs. Such a move can dismantle your entire carefully constructed plan. If you're selling in a slump, not only do you lock in your losses, but also you risk being out of the market when it's time to take advantage of the run-ups.

Don't Be Guided by Mr. Market

Warren Buffett credits his friend and teacher Benjamin Graham with a parable about investment success:

> [Graham] said that you should imagine market quotations as coming from a remarkably accommodating fellow named Mr. Market who is your partner in a private business. Without fail, Mr. Market appears daily and names a price at which he will either buy your interest or sell you his.
>
> Even though the business that the two of you own may have economic characteristics that are stable, Mr. Market's quotations will be anything but. For, sad to say, the poor fellow has incurable emotional problems. At times he feels euphoric and can see only the favorable factors affecting the business. When in that mood, he names a very high buy-sell price because he fears that you will snap up his interest and rob him of imminent gains. At other times he is depressed and can see nothing but trouble ahead for both the business and the world. On these occasions he will name a very low price, since he is terrified that you will unload your interest on him.
>
> Mr. Market has another endearing characteristic: He doesn't mind being ignored. If his quotation is uninteresting to you today, he will be back with a new one tomorrow. Transactions are strictly

at your option. Under these conditions, the more manic-depressive his behavior, the better for you.

But, like Cinderella at the ball, you must heed one warning or everything will turn into pumpkins and mice: Mr. Market is there to serve you, not to guide you. It is his pocketbook, not his wisdom, that you will find useful. If he shows up some day in a particularly foolish mood, you are free to either ignore him or to take advantage of him, but it will be disastrous if you fall under his influence. Indeed, if you aren't certain that you understand and can value your business far better than Mr. Market, you don't belong in the game. As they say in poker, "If you've been in the game 30 minutes and you don't know who the patsy is, *you're* the patsy."*

Mr. Market isn't wise; he just has a huge bankroll and is always ready to trade. But if you take his lead—if you view him as smart rather than recognizing that he's bipolar—you're likely to be out of the market at just the time you need to be in.

If you know the role of your investments in your portfolio, you won't let your buy or sell decisions be guided by Mr. Market's mercurial nature. Stocks are never priced exactly right. They're always priced too high or too low. It's unrealistic to think you will be able to sell at the high or buy at the bottom. Rather than be whipsawed by Mr. Market's mood of the day, you have to know why holding or unloading an investment at any particular time makes sense for your particular portfolio.

Risk and Volatility Are Different

I've used this Mr. Market parable to demonstrate how volatility affects your psyche. By now, you should be aware of how the media relies on Mr. Market's mood swings to create the headlines of the day. You've seen that to benefit from the fact that when one sector zigs another will zag, the solution is asset allocation. Finally and most important, you should internalize the message that risk and volatility are cousins but not twins. Risk is a gauge of how likely you are to reach your desired outcome, and volatility is about how bumpy the ride will be.

---

* Online at www.berkshirehathaway.com/letters/1987.html.

As I write this, I think of my recent experience with a client whose financial needs exceed the amount of money she could earn in investing in a bond portfolio alone. To meet those needs, I explained to her, she has to accept a certain amount of volatility. She understood my explanation, and ultimately she agreed to a plan with a modest level of risk built into it.

But when the market started going down, she had a terrible time. She'd been prepared for the fact that there were going to be volatile periods, but she panicked and at one point contemplated selling everything and putting the money under the mattress. Fortunately, she stayed the course. She was able to hang onto the lesson that Figure 7.3 makes clear.

Each of the five charts tracks volatility on a rolling basis from the years 1926 to 2009. The first chart has been tremendously compressed in size, because what it tracks is how much the S&P 500 moved **monthly** (with gains or losses expressed in percentiles) every single month for that 84-year period. The chart looks like an EKG, with peaks and valleys occurring with dizzying frequency.

The second chart tracks the **annual** market performance of the S&P 500 in one-year periods. While there is still a lot of movement up and down, the movement is not nearly as erratic as on the monthly chart.

The third chart tracks what happened over any given **five-year** interval, all the way from 1926 to 2009. It's a rolling average: The first entry records what happened from 1926 to 1930, the next from 1927 to 1931, all the way through 2005–2009. When you look at this chart, the picture begins to look very different. You see that there are only 11 five-year cycles (mostly around the Depression) where you would have had a negative return in the S&P 500, and the losses would have been small compared to the gains.

The chart tracking **10-year** intervals shows there were only four such cycles when stocks would have shown even modest negative returns, two at the time of the Great Depression and the two 10-year periods ending in 2008 and 2009. When you look at a chart of **15-year** intervals, you will see no down cycles at all.

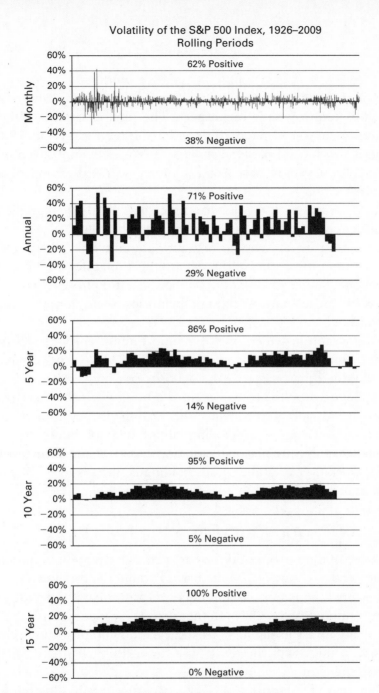

Figure 7.3 Time Frame Can Change Your Perception

Source: Ibbotson® SBBI® 2010 Classic Yearbook. © 2010 Morningstar. All rights reserved. Used with permission. Performance of the S&P 500 stock index, 1926–2009.

The first chart, with its dramatic swings, shows the kind of angst the short-term investor can expect. The final chart shows that no matter when you entered the market during the period 1926 to 2009, if you looked past the short-term volatility and stayed in, the less likely you were to have lost any money over that extended period of time.

Understanding the role that time plays is a key ingredient to investment success and to reclaiming your nest egg. Naturally, you monitor your investments to take into account what's happening in real time; but the events of the short term should not be the impetus to bail out. Rather, they should be the inspiration to see if your game plan is still an accurate reflection of your needs and, if not, to change it accordingly.

As a wealth manager, one of my most important jobs is persuading my clients to take that message to heart. One of my clients says that the role I play is exactly the opposite of a lifeguard's.

A lifeguard pulls people out of the pool when they fear they're drowning. My job is to convince them to stay in—even to stomp on their fingers when they try to climb out of the pool. I do that because I know that if your personal situation hasn't changed and you let capital work over multiple cycles, holding equities is overwhelmingly a rewarding choice.

You Can't Time the Market

The fable of the tortoise and the hare gets our attention because deep down, everyone wants to be the hare. Though the tortoise is the ultimate winner, he is not a role model we easily adopt. Currently, after having endured two of only four negative 10-year periods for the S&P 500, many investors are anxious and even downright skeptical about staying on track with the tenacity of the tortoise. It's hard for them to keep the faith.

But consider Figure 7.4. The chart graphically illustrates that for the past 60 years, not only have markets stayed in bull phase for much longer than in bear phase, but also the upsides are much stronger.

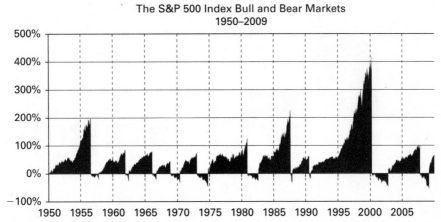

Figure 7.4 Bull Markets Are Stronger and Last Longer Than Bear Markets

Source: Yahoo! Finance. Data represents percentage changes in the S&P 500 index and does not take into consideration the effects of dividends.

Compare the width and rise of the bull market phases above the line to the narrowness and shallowness of the bear market phases below the line. Now you see why the longer cycles produce such good overall results. The relatively short and shallow dips of the bear periods will steal the wealth created by the longer and more substantial rises of bull periods only if you let it.

Still, though they are short and less dramatic, those bear periods rattle people disproportionately. I like to use an analogy to your teeth. You don't think about them when they're doing what they're supposed to: chewing your food and not creating any problems.

But when you have a toothache, you can think of nothing but making the pain stop. When investments create that kind of intense and relentless pain, the way people get it to stop is by selling everything and getting out of the market.

Figure 7.5 shows that in the 15 years from 1995 through the end of 2009, the S&P 500 index's annualized total return was 8.0 percent. If you weren't invested during the 10 best performance days

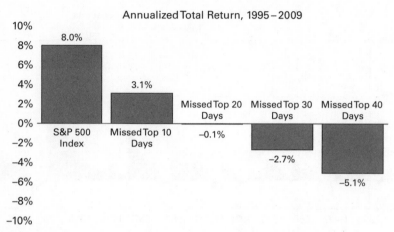

Figure 7.5 Time in the Market Is More Important Than Timing the Market
Source: Mercadien Asset Management.

during that period, your portfolio went up only 3.1 percent. And if you missed the top 40 days, you lost an annualized 5.1 percent.

In that 15-year period, 73 percent of the best days in the market occurred within two weeks of the market's worst days. If you leave during the toothache period, you're unlikely to jump back in right away—which practically guarantees you're going to miss the big run-ups and recoveries.

You have to stay focused on the long-term risks of your investment decisions rather than the short-term volatility of the market movement.

Diversify, Don't Duplicate

Being diversified means holding a true mixture of investments, but some investors get tripped up by what I call phantom diversification. Often, the problem is just a matter of failing to understand where they're putting their money.

After the debacle of 2008, I was contacted by a prospective client whose portfolio had been thoroughly beaten up. He told me he was an exceedingly conservative investor, not interested in chasing big returns but just committed to steady growth, and he couldn't understand why he'd been pummeled so badly.

I looked over his portfolio, and I realized right away what had happened. He had taken what he thought was the prudent step of putting his assets almost entirely into mutual funds—17 of them, all focused around the companies represented by the S&P 500—and in addition, he individually owned several blue-chip stocks. Over the years, whenever he heard about some new top-performing fund, he'd gather up some cash and buy into it, figuring that not only was he getting a piece of the latest and greatest, but also he was further diversifying. All good, right?

He failed to connect the dots and realize that those top-performing funds, the ones that were making the news, were doing so well because each of them was heavily weighted in financial stocks, which were for a few years the darlings of the market. As a result, the holdings of virtually all of his mutual funds overlapped not only with the individual blue-chip stocks he was holding—most of them financials—but also with one another.

When I ran an attribution report, which showed the internal makeup of his combined portfolios, I was able to show him the extent of the overlap. Most of the funds were totally redundant on the top 20 holdings, and that redundancy effectively wiped out any benefit from the diversification below the top 20. It wasn't sufficient to smooth out the ride. When the financials crashed, his entire portfolio took a huge hit.

What he had thought was a conservative, well-diversified portfolio was in fact highly aggressive, since his fortunes were substantially linked to a narrow sector. This investor had made a couple of classic mistakes at the same time. He chased performance, and he didn't look under the covers to see how his mutual funds were investing. He had a bunch of different managers, but they were all trolling in the same waters.

If you're in a single category, no matter how many stocks or funds you own, you're not effectively diversifying; in fact, there's a very good chance you're duplicating. And having all your money in a single silo in my opinion is as aggressive as you get. True diversification is having investments in multiple asset classes, so that whichever one is in favor, you're participating.

Diversification Isn't Insulation

Asset allocation is a winning long-term strategy, but it's not going to shield you from occasional setbacks. As I've pointed out, even when you're looking at an overall long-term upward slope of the market, once you zero in more closely you'll always find a sawtooth pattern with a lot of ups and downs.

When you're going through those moves to the downside, you'll always find them traumatic. But it's a lot easier to shake them off if you keep in mind that you're never going to lock in every upward move; that all those ups and downs are part of the process; and that in fact moving three steps forward and two steps back is actually part of the plan—not necessarily welcomed, but certainly anticipated.

It's true that after the debacle of 2008, a lot of people felt they were let down by asset allocation. Everyone started running for the doors. People wanted their money back no matter where it was invested, and all asset classes came down at the same time. But that was a real anomaly.

Such a perfect storm, where everything is driven by extreme fear, is extremely rare. It's as infrequent as Halley's Comet, which comes along about once in 70 years. You can't run your financial future paralyzed about a situation that historically has proven to be a rare event.

On the other hand, if you don't anticipate any discomfort, you're having false expectations. You're not applying the theory correctly, and you're at risk to bolt at some point rather than sit out the long term. Know those dips will happen, expect them to happen, and have a framework to deal with them. That means you have to stop thinking in terms of dollars.

When you're making your calculations in dollars, whenever the market goes down, you'll be working out your angst in terms of what you might have bought: *I could have bought those shoes I coveted. I should have sprung for the vacation in France. Why the heck didn't I go ahead with plans for the new media room?*

A client with a $6 million portfolio bemoaned the fact she was down 4 percent. "You're cursed by your blessings," I told her. "You're having so much anxiety because you have so much money." That 4 percent downturn, for her, represented almost a quarter of a million dollars. True, that's a big number.

But during the period in question, the market was down 8 percent and she was down only 4 percent. Her asset allocation was working. It didn't eliminate all the bumps in the ride, but it certainly softened them. However, thinking in dollars gave her a flawed perspective.

There are a lot of theories about why people with a lot of money often don't seem as happy as they should be, most of them involving a psychological explanation. But I think a lot of it can be attributed to a much less complicated reason: They just get so stressed out watching huge sums of money making huge swings.

One of my clients started out in the garment business, and he tells me that the weekly fluctuation in his current account represents more money than he routinely took home in an entire year. As people get older they become a prisoner to their money because they are stuck in dollar terms. I tell clients like this that they have to develop a philosophy of percentages.

If you don't think in terms of percentages, here's what happens: If your portfolio is invested properly and things go according to plan, your money should grow. And when that happens, your angst will multiply, since the dollar swings will become greater and greater. While 3 percent of $100,000 is just $3,000, 3 percent of $10 million is $300,000.

To develop a stick-to-it attitude you need to be unemotional. Looking at what you're doing in terms of percentages rather than dollar amounts helps you think about your budget and investment goals more evenhandedly and rationally: *What percentage of my money can I spend per year?* and *What percentage should my money grow annually to achieve that goal?* are the questions to ask when you're thinking in terms of your lifestyle.

Don't Set It and Forget It

The only way to see if your plan is working is to raise your head out of your foxhole and take a look around. Is what you put in place reacting in line with what's going on all around? That's your real concern.

Suppose the market is up 10 percent and your overall portfolio is up 5 percent. If only half your portfolio is invested in equities, then you're probably right on track. But if you're 100 percent in equities and up only 5 percent when the market is up 10 percent, that's a sign to reevaluate your asset allocation decisions.

Most growing things need attention: your child, your garden, and also your nest egg. The real world changes; your financial situation changes; fund managers come and go. Even though you're investing long-term, you have to readjust the plans.

Every year, do a checkup to make sure that the choices you made in various asset classes are still appropriate and you're on the path to your goals. To determine whether your investment decisions need adjusting, benchmark your results against the market indices.

Taxes Aren't Your First Concern

My grandfather used to tell me that my goal should be to pay a lot of taxes, because paying a lot of taxes would mean I was making a lot of money. Paying taxes is a necessary obligation in our society, and it's also a measure of your success. But don't get me wrong: While the number one goal in investing is to make money, the secondary goal is to retain as much as you can—and the professional in me is always looking for opportunities to minimize the tax consequences.

However, in order to increase your assets, sometimes paying taxes is necessary. It may be a big mistake to hold onto a stock that's had a huge rise rather than pay the capital gains tax that a sale would trigger. An individual I know watched AIG go up and up and up. What kept him invested was thinking about the huge tax bill he'd owe Uncle Sam once he cashed out.

His concerns about the tax bill eclipsed any of his concerns about the company's fundamentals, and he left his financial future heavily dependent on the fortunes of a single company. When everyone was blindsided by the revelations that the company was so distressed, and AIG was wiped out, Uncle Sam wound up with nothing; but so did he.

No doubt plenty of others learned the same lesson in 2008, having allowed themselves to be held hostage to large, concentrated positions in their portfolios because they didn't want to pay the tax man.

Other people, often mature, wealthy individuals, are so averse to paying taxes that they buy only tax-free bonds. As a result, so much of their income may be tax-free that they're in a very low tax bracket. An analysis of the portfolios of such a client may reveal that if they invest in higher-yielding corporate bonds—just enough to keep them below the threshold of the next higher tax bracket—their total portfolio would be earning more money on an after-tax basis.

Don't Buy on Margin

Accelerating your upside possibility isn't the goal in retirement planning because doing so accelerates your downside possibility exponentially. Don't even consider leveraging or buying on margin. Margin buyers were among the first to get crushed in the downturn.

Just consider this: You've put up $10 and borrowed $10 from the brokerage firm to buy a $20 stock. Suppose it moves up 100 percent and now is worth $40. You pay back the $10, and you have $30 left. True, you've made a 200 percent return on your original investment.

But suppose instead that the $20 stock goes down to $10. It's gone down by only 50 percent, but you have to pay the remaining $10 back to the person you borrowed it from—and you are left with nothing.

Borrowing money can supersize your pain because leveraging puts your risk on steroids.

Avoid Illiquid Investments

At the stage when you're looking to reclaim your nest egg, you don't want to have to wait to get your money, so don't make inappropriate investments with money that you may need for tactical moves. It's not only high-risk gambles that are inappropriate but also investments that you can't easily turn into cash.

Many people were hurt in the aftermath of 2008 because they had money tied up so that access was slow or, worse, it was totally unavailable for an extended period. If they didn't have enough dry powder, they were forced to sell off whatever they could to raise money. That triggered unwelcome tax consequences or forced them to divest investments at deeply depressed prices.

In some cases, the money was tied up in collectibles like Chippendale furniture or Dali paintings. Some of these items might even have appreciated while the stock market was going down, but it wasn't easy to sell them. Before the meltdown, a friend of mine who collects Americana would simply put a Remington up for sale when he needed cash, but after 2008, he's had trouble finding buyers.

The market for collectibles is limited to individuals who have the wealth and inclination to buy luxury items. Hard times means that there are fewer of them, and some may even be having liquidity problems of their own.

Real estate is another illiquid category. Prior to 2008, many people had become overnight real estate moguls. But once the downturn began, many of them were holding onto properties that they couldn't sell or even rent. I counseled one individual in a mortgage limited partnership that allowed him to remove only one-twelfth of his money quarterly. He was able to get back his money eventually, but it took three years.

Another kind of illiquid investment is a hedge fund. The allure of buying into a hedge fund is that you're "in on" something. Hedge fund operators, who shroud their strategies in secrecy, operate like the Wizard of Oz. Buying into a black box investment—the kind of secret that's a secret even to you—is a questionable move.

You're buying the promise of a return, but you don't know how the holdings overlap with your other planning, and there's no way to assess the fund's future prospects. You never get a peek behind the curtain. I've been driving home the point that you have to know what you're holding, so I'm no fan of this sort of investment philosophically. What's more, there's no way to make a hasty exit and cash out of a hedge fund on your own schedule.

Stay on Top of Everything

In a post–Bernie Madoff world, I don't think I need to spend a lot of time convincing you to read your statements, be certain you understand what you own, and make sure your statements come from a recognized financial institution that is regularly audited by banking or security regulators.

Now that you have your investment philosophy and the rules of the road, you can get down to constructing a portfolio.

Key Takeaways

- **Having no plan is a plan.** Even in the absence of guidelines, you're obliged to make financial decisions. The result is a series of haphazard, short-term choices that may be contradictory and even destructive. First you need goals and then you have to figure out how you'll achieve them.
- **Define your investment guidelines.** Making decisions on the fly, based on current events and the emotions of the moment, can be catastrophic to your long-term success. Establishing operating rules will help you as an investor in the same way they do in any other enterprise where you're pursuing long-term goals.
- **Playing it too safe can be dangerous.** To keep pace with inflation, it's essential that your assets grow, and historically the best way to achieve growth has been by investing in equities. In fact, including equities among your investments can make your portfolio more conservative by decreasing volatility and increasing return.
- **_When_ you need money dictates _where_ to put it.** For this year's bills, leave your money in cash. Money to pay for next year's car purchase or college bills should be in short-term, interest-paying investments. But money for your nest egg can be exposed

to the volatility of the market, since the longer your time horizon, the more likely it is that you'll meet your goal.

■ **Make sure you're as diversified as you believe you are.** Mutual funds attract customers by appearing unique. They give themselves distinctive names and write brochures that make it appear that they're pursuing differing goals. But many of them have similar positions. Always look at the top 30 or so holdings of any mutual fund before you buy so you don't fall into the trap of "phantom diversification"—investing in funds that own many of the same companies although in different wrappers.

■ **To serve you a lifetime, your plan needs continual monitoring.** While it is important to stick to your core principles, you have to keep your plan relevant and responsive to shifts in external, real-world variables. Those include macro changes (revisions to the tax law, global economic changes) and changes in your own situation (health status, long-term goals, etc.).

8

Reconstruct
Your Portfolio

YOU NEED A PORTFOLIO that will stand the test of time, but the one you've got may be good for only a few seasons.

To review what you've got, start by thinking about whether you're well diversified. Should you simply add to what you already have, or do you need to start from scratch?

You might feel comfortable analyzing some investment categories on your own, but no one knows everything. In the process of putting together a new or revised portfolio, the chances are you'll need assistance in compiling a shopping list. So your next step is deciding what form that assistance should take.

Man or Machine: Who Calls the Shots?

Are you going to rely on the straightforward and cost-effective operation of computers to select the securities that comprise your asset allocation, or are you inclined to seek out the experience and intellect of professionals?

If you want to own everything in an asset class, you are likely to be interested in indexing, which is the term for buying exposure to an entire sector. For example, to acquire large cap companies, you might buy the S&P 500 fund; to acquire mid-cap companies, the S&P MidCap 400 fund; to acquire small-cap companies, the Russell 2000 fund, and so on. And the way to own entire sectors today is by using computers.

As the names indicate, each index has a set number of securities. The computer that manages the index fund is programmed to match the index portfolio exactly, so if the Russell 2000 index drops 40 companies and replaces them with another 40, the fund's computer does the same.

This approach is called passive investing. No individual is trying to weigh the relative merits of any particular security over another. You have only to decide what sectors you want to be exposed to and in what amount, and after that, the process is mechanical and automatic.

If you believe no manager or management group can perform better than the market as a whole, then this is the approach you would choose. Its chief advantage is that the fees are small, since the costs of programming and maintaining computers are much lower than paying managers' salaries. If cost is the primary factor in making your decisions, owning indexes is the way to go.

The disadvantage of passive investing is that you're giving up any opportunity of enhanced returns. And that's why some people prefer active management, which means having managers pick and choose the securities. If it were impossible to do better than computers, the financial services industry as we know it would cease to exist. The managers' job is to capture opportunities by determining whether securities are priced too high or too low, a process known as price discovery.

If there were no reasons to choose the stock of one company over another, their relative values would not fluctuate. So to dismiss the notion of active management is to dismiss the entire history of the stock market before computerization. To make distinctions—to favor one equity or bond over another, to see treasure where someone else sees trash—you have to perceive relative value. Otherwise, markets would move like the tide, rising collectively when investors add money to the pool and receding when capital is withdrawn.

Advocates of active management believe that an experienced manager with sound investment principles can keep you away from places you shouldn't be and find opportunities that get diluted by owning entire indexes. For example, in 2008, the Russell 2000 plunged dramatically. Can you assume that all 2,000 companies remained strong enough to rebound, let alone stay in business?

The philosophy of active management is that it's possible to enhance your portfolio returns by selling what's overvalued and buying up more of what's undervalued—perhaps even your former holdings, once they come down in price. You pay a higher fee for active management, betting on the intellectual firepower of people with expertise in particular sectors to make a selection of securities that they believe will outperform the sector as a whole.

Being an active or passive investor doesn't rise to the level of a religious conviction. You may use a mix. In some segments, you might be comfortable using passive management and in others you might prefer to have someone thinking things through.

Sleepers and Sizzlers

Most companies usually fit into one of two categories. An attention-grabbing sizzler—expanding faster and achieving greater market share than its peers—is considered a *growth* stock. A less exciting sleeper—trading at a lower market valuation than its comparable competitors—is considered a *value* stock. That's the difference in a nutshell.

Shares of a company are perceived as growth stock when the company is outpacing its competitors because its prospects are hot. Think Microsoft when it was brand new, or Apple, which was initially hot, then slipped, but reclaimed its position as a growth company with the introduction of the iPod and other innovative products.

Growth companies are likely to be reinvesting earnings into new plants, new equipment, or an expanding work force—whatever is needed to fuel the company's expansion—so investors forgo dividends in expectation of growth, greater sales, and eventually, greater earnings.

For obvious reasons, growth companies tend to be more volatile. A growth company has no laurels to rest on and stays in favor by remaining fresh and ahead of the curve. If it fails to keep up the pace and loses its edge, another company will soon take its spot as the market darling.

Shares of a company are viewed as value stock when they're selling for a bargain price relative to their intrinsic worth (based on dividends, earnings, sales, etc.) and in comparison to the price of the stock of similar companies. A short-term blip—legal problems, a poor earnings report, or negative publicity—may push a company's stock into the value category. Bad news that affects one company may even rock an entire sector, turning some competitors' stocks into value stocks by painting them with the same brush.

For example, in 1982, seven people died after taking Tylenol that had been poisoned with potassium chloride. The incident led eventually to tamper-proof packaging, but the initial blizzard of negative stories in the media affected not only the stock of Johnson & Johnson, the manufacturer of Tylenol (whose market share dove 29 percent before it eventually recovered), but also all the other pharmaceuticals.

Many companies whose stock would fall into the value category are mature organizations. They may generate a lot of cash that they don't need to pump back into the company in order to grow. These companies are more likely to return a portion of the profits as dividends to stockholders.

Coca-Cola is a good example. It may not be a trendsetter or an exciting growth prospect because it's already achieved worldwide market penetration. On the other hand, though not easily quantified on a balance sheet, its global presence and tremendous name recognition add a great deal of worth to the brand.

But what really attracts people to invest in a company whose stock is categorized as value is the expectation that some sort of catalytic event will unlock that value, causing the price to appreciate. Without such a catalyst, some companies may trade cheaper than their peers for decades, causing what some analysts refer to as investing in a "value trap."

There are no hard and fast rules determining what makes a growth or value company. Often, it's a matter of perception. Depending on what is going on in the world and with the company itself, shares in a single company may at one time be characterized as growth and at another as value—and even as both at the same time. Making the judgment call is one of the things a manager is hired to do.

How Do You Buy It?

There are various ways to purchase the market segments that a well-diversified allocation model calls for. In equities, for example, you need to select among companies of varying size, international stocks, and value and growth companies or a blend. And to allocate in fixed income, you have to choose between putting your money into corporate or government bonds, taxable or tax-free bonds.

You might, as I've suggested, want to make your own selections in one or two sectors. If you plan to hold your bonds to maturity, you might feel there's little need for management, or you may have your own ideas about what large-cap companies to buy. You can also buy bond and equity investments in any of the modalities described below.

You are probably familiar with the concept of *mutual funds*, which exist in every style-box category—equity, fixed income, commodities, and so on—as well as in distinct subcategories such as value, growth or blend, international or domestic, passive or active.

All index funds are passive funds. The fund will match the return of the index very closely though not exactly, since the share price includes management fees and the models for sampling and mirroring, by their nature, might not be 100 percent accurate.

Many mutual fund companies offer index funds, but the majority of them are in business to offer services in actively managed funds that put together a select group of securities in various industries, styles, and sectors. To choose a fund, look at its track record—a historical demonstration that the manager (or management group) has a handle on that section of the market and does indeed enhance portfolio returns over time.

Whatever the investment mandate, index and managed funds work the same way: You send your investment to the fund manager, who adds your money to the pool. You are issued shares that represent a portion of all the securities that the fund acquires. As more dollars come in from other investors, a manager has to buy more securities, and when investors cash out, the manager has to sell. The shares are priced daily, based on the total net asset value (NAV) of the fund's holdings at 4:00 P.M., when the market closes. Administrative and management fees are built into the share price.

There are three ways to get a return on your mutual fund investments. Income produced by the securities (dividends from stock, interest from bonds) is distributed among investors. If the fund sells securities and makes a profit on the sale, this capital gain is also distributed to investors. And if the fund retains holdings that have increased in price, then the fund's shares increase in price and you may sell them for a profit.

One major advantage to using mutual funds rather than making your own picks is, of course, professional assistance. Managed diversification—spreading your risk among various companies—is another.

Other than costs, the downsides include dilution. The term refers to the fact that funds with small holdings in a great many companies may be overdiversified, so that even if a few companies do very well, the net effect to each shareholder becomes almost insignificant. Also, when popular funds get too big, the managers may have trouble finding productive places to invest money.

Tax consequences may be a bigger issue. The tax basis for your purchase is established the day on which you entered the fund, but you are also responsible for the embedded taxes the fund owes for purchases it made prior to your buying in.

So if a fund bought a security 10 years ago that is currently up 1,000 percent and the managers decide to sell it the day after you buy in, you are responsible for paying the pro rata share of the capital gains tax incurred internally by the fund. Your tax obligation will be calculated just as if you had owned the appreciated security for 10 years.

During 2008, when many funds were down dramatically, the fund managers were defensively selling positions to lock in their gains or were under pressure to raise funds to pay the investors who wanted to cash out. They were forced to sell long-held, greatly appreciated securities, triggering huge embedded capital gains taxes that affected all shareholders.

In some cases, this added tremendous insult to injury. An investor who saw her mutual fund sink 40 percent might also be hit by the large tax bill for "gains" that didn't benefit her if she had bought into the fund only a short time before.

An *exchange-traded fund (ETF)* works like a mutual fund. But instead of being priced at the close of the market, they're traded like stocks, all day long. ETFs are a favorite investment medium of day traders—"gamblers" who trade in and out of the market to capitalize on every bit of news and minute movement. Buying them for retirement planning, your intent would be to stay in them long term rather than use them for intraday trading or to speculate.

Since almost all ETFs are index funds, they can be a very useful means to hold broad asset classes without management assistance. In many cases, ETFs may be less costly than traditional mutual funds and by design are usually very tax efficient.

For a more customized portfolio, you can choose a *separately managed account (SMA)*. SMAs are to mutual funds as limousines are to buses—a customized rather than a group way to get you where you want to go. Typically, you need an investment account worth at least $500,000.

With the SMA approach, you (or your advisor acting on your behalf) hire managers to start an account for you and to function like mutual fund managers. (In fact, many mutual fund companies also manage accounts separately.) The managers are specialists in particular areas—large-cap, small-cap, international, and so on—and whom you choose depends on your allocation plans.

Using the mutual fund approach, if you diversify into a group of style boxes, you might be holding 10 or 15 funds. But using separate accounts, you typically might have five or six managers each buying 30 to 50 individual securities, for a total of perhaps 300 holdings.

With an SMA, you pay a flat fee, so while there may be a lot of trading, that won't drive up your costs. And there are several benefits to an SMA. One is performance potential. While the average mutual fund holds hundreds of securities, most of their return might come from the top 50. You won't be holding legacy positions or other under-performing securities when you're running your own SMA. Your manager can create a portfolio with just his top 50 ideas.

In addition, you can monitor overlap more closely. On their statements, mutual fund clients will see only the names of the five or 10 funds they hold. The statement for the SMA investor will list each of the equity positions and values separately. (The total value of the account will be the aggregate value of the positions.) There is no "phantom diversification" because you know right away if you're holding the same securities in different accounts.

A third advantage is being able to manage the tax implications of your investments. If there's a large gain to be realized by selling one security, you can offset it by selling other holdings where you can take a loss.

Finally, you can customize the selection of stocks in your portfolio depending on your philosophy, enthusiasms, or other criteria. If you're an executive in a specific industry—pharmaceuticals, say—your manager can stay away from related investments since (presuming you hold company stock) you already have exposure in that area. If you're philosophically opposed to smoking, you can stay out of tobacco-related investments; and if you're ardently green, you can choose only eco-friendly investments.

Sample Portfolios

The next few pages illustrate a broad approach for customers of different temperaments and then how portfolios might be customized for hypothetical clients—and why.

What these samples should make obvious is that there are no absolutes in terms of investment recommendations. Though people may say that their investment temperament is conservative, aggressive, or somewhere in-between, that is only a starting point. Creating a specific portfolio means taking into account many factors, including age, marital status, family responsibilities, employment status, total of assets, and life goals.

The examples shown are not meant to be recommendations or templates but simply examples of what to think about in constructing your own portfolio.

Prototypical Conservative Allocation

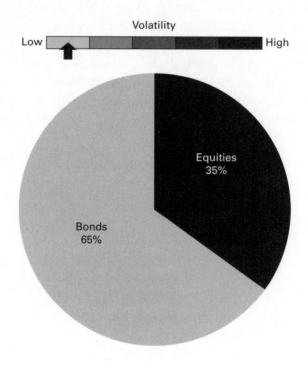

Portfolio Objective	Capital preservation plus current income
Portfolio Characteristics	Controlled volatility Current income Lower long-term growth potential Lower potential inflation protection
Allocation Considerations	Equity allocation to provide growth potential to offer some inflation protection Equity allocation should:

- Focus on companies with solid balance sheets and proven track records
- Maintain moderate exposure to fast-growing small- and mid-sized companies

Bond allocation overweighted to reduce volatility and provide a steady stream of income.
Bond allocation should be:

- Well-diversified by maturities to manage interest rate risk
- Well-diversified by issuers to manage credit default risk

Investor Profile Someone who:

- Prefers stability over growth
- Has a low tolerance for volatility
- Relies on portfolio income to support his or her lifestyle
- Has capital that cannot remain invested for long-term market cycles

Suggested Conservative Allocation

Client: "Arnold Keller"

Portfolio Size: $1,000,000

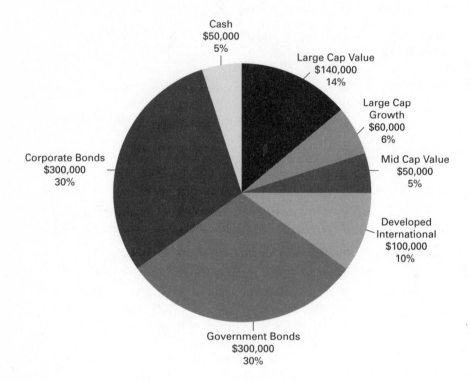

Cash
$50,000
5%

Large Cap Value
$140,000
14%

Large Cap
Growth
$60,000
6%

Corporate Bonds
$300,000
30%

Mid Cap Value
$50,000
5%

Developed
International
$100,000
10%

Government Bonds
$300,000
30%

Profile of Arnold Keller

Arnold Keller, 76 and a widower, is a retired manufacturing engineer. Arnold is very fit, an avid hiker and ardent traveler who likes to take two or three high-end guided tours to exotic destinations each year. He visits his three sons and their families often and prides himself on having the ability to help them out financially should the need arise.

Income Needs

In order to maintain his current lifestyle, Arnold needs to withdraw $5,000 per month from his portfolio—a 6 percent withdrawal rate—to augment his other sources of income (a pension and Social Security).

Investment Sentiment

Having witnessed his parents' struggles with money when he was a young boy, Arnold is fearful of having the market "steal" the fruits of his life's labor. As a result, he monitors the markets on a daily basis. Although he knows he shouldn't track the ups and downs so closely, watching the business channels has become a big part of his daily routine, causing what he admits is a significant amount of stress.

Investment Objective

While Arnold would love to leave as much as possible to his children, his primary concern is to maintain his current retirement lifestyle. He anticipates that age and deteriorating health will at some point curb his wanderlust, thus reducing his future portfolio withdrawal needs.

Recommendation

A conservative, low-volatility allocation makes sense for Arnold, given his conservative investment sentiment and reliance on portfolio income. His 6 percent withdrawal rate is fairly high. On an inflation-adjusted basis, maintaining such a rate of withdrawal poses a risk that he may outlive his assets. But Arnold's age, the likelihood his travel expenses will diminish, and the fact that he has a "keep the change" attitude toward legacy, mitigate those concerns.

Suggested Conservative Allocation

Clients: "Dr. Salvatore and Carmen Lorenzo"

Portfolio Size: $5,000,000

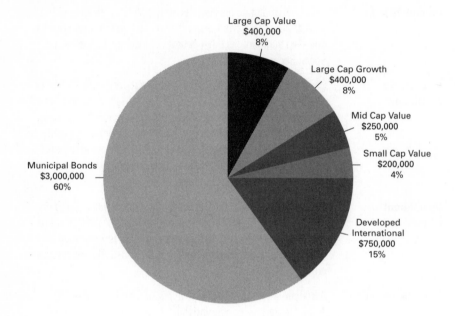

Large Cap Value
$400,000
8%

Large Cap Growth
$400,000
8%

Mid Cap Value
$250,000
5%

Small Cap Value
$200,000
4%

Developed
International
$750,000
15%

Municipal Bonds
$3,000,000
60%

Profile of Dr. Salvatore and Carmen Lorenzo

Dr. Salvatore Lorenzo, 62, anticipates winding down his medical practice in three years. At that point, he and his wife, Carmen, 63, who is a volunteer, plan to spend a lot of time at their beach house, where they keep their boat. Bought when their children were young and expanded over the years, the house is big enough to accommodate their three children and their families, whom they hope will visit often.

Income Needs

Dr. Lorenzo intends to work part-time at the local hospital after leaving his private practice to keep his skills sharp and to bring in some extra income. Adding this to the income from his portfolio makes tax management a priority. The Lorenzos anticipate needing to withdraw $150,000 per year from the portfolio—a 3 percent withdrawal rate—to maintain their current lifestyle.

Investment Sentiment

The couple has built a moderate equity portfolio and handled market volatility very well. Nevertheless, Dr. and Mrs. Lorenzo say they would prefer to have greater certainty regarding cash flow and don't want to push for higher rates of return, since that would expose them to greater market volatility.

Investment Objective

The Lorenzos have amassed more money than they contemplate spending during their retirement years. Their goal is to enjoy the fruits of their labors and leave a legacy for their children and grandchildren.

Recommendation

While a conservative allocation is probably overly cautious in this case, it accomplishes the clients' goals: to have a highly predictable cash flow and to build a legacy for their heirs. The portfolio could effectively be considered in two parts: a fixed allocation to meet retirement income needs and an equity allocation to achieve growth for their heirs. The fixed allocation should be in municipal bonds, since in their high tax bracket they would benefit from the tax-free income they provide. The equity allocation can be more aggressive, since it's being invested for children and grandchildren, with a long time horizon.

Prototypical Balanced Allocation

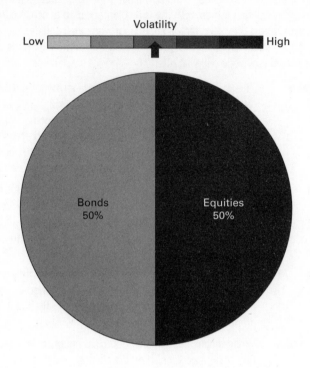

Portfolio Objective	Balance the needs of capital appreciation and current income
Portfolio Characteristics	Moderate volatility Relatively moderate current income Moderate long-term growth potential Moderate potential inflation protection
Allocation Considerations	Equity allocation should:

Equity allocation should:

- Provide the opportunity for capital appreciation
- Avoid concentration risk from a specific asset class
- Be positioned to participate in worldwide growth opportunities

Bond allocation should:

- Provide a steady stream of income
- Be well-diversified by maturities to manage interest rate risk
- Be well-diversified by issuers to manage credit default risk

Investor Profile Someone who:

- Requires both growth and steady income
- Accepts moderate volatility in order to achieve long-term goals
- Wants to satisfy both current income needs and maintain long-term purchasing power
- Needs to maintain level of growth to accommodate future spending needs

Suggested Balanced Allocation

Client: "Janet Ford"

Portfolio Size: $3,500,000

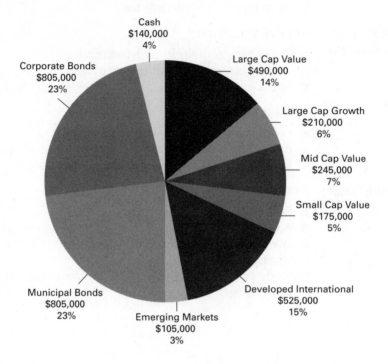

Profile of Janet Ford

Janet Ford, 52, a former preschool teacher, was recently widowed when her 55-year-old husband, Phillip, died of cancer. The sole breadwinner, he left a large insurance policy plus savings and separate funding for college tuitions. At the moment, Janet is remaining at home to care for her children, Geoffrey, 16, beginning his junior year of high school, and Juliet, 20, about to enter her junior year in college.

Income Needs

While Janet intends to return to the work force at some point in the future, she is currently entirely reliant on the portfolio to produce the $150,000 per year—a 3 percent withdrawal rate—she needs to run her household. Furthermore, she anticipates that her mother, Dorothy, 70 and in deteriorating health, may need to move in with her in the coming years. Should that occur, Janet anticipates her withdrawal needs will climb to $175,000 per year— a 5 percent withdrawal rate—to cover her mother's basic costs and some household help. In a few years, when her children have graduated and left home, her withdrawal needs are anticipated to drop.

Investment Sentiment

Janet was rarely involved with making major financial decisions prior to her husband's death. Now, considering the financial demands of supporting herself, her children, and her mother, she is very stressed. She considers herself neither conservative nor aggressive. Her only concern is keeping her nest egg intact.

Investment Objective

Janet wants to balance her current and anticipated income requirements with enough growth to hedge the effects of inflation over her expected lifespan. She would like to see her portfolio weather her short-term high withdrawals, while she cares for her mother and children, with enough left over to maintain the comfortable lifestyle she had expected as the wife of a successful businessman.

Recommendation

While Janet's personal retirement income needs are manageable, her need to care for her mother and possibly help her kids get their "start" creates a need for a balanced but somewhat growth-oriented portfolio. It has to accommodate the early high withdrawal years while attempting to ensure her future purchasing power.

Suggested Balanced Allocation

Client: "Leon and Sharon Washington"
Portfolio Size: $250,000

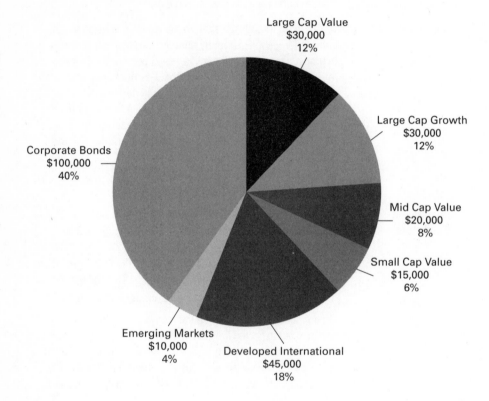

Large Cap Value
$30,000
12%

Large Cap Growth
$30,000
12%

Mid Cap Value
$20,000
8%

Small Cap Value
$15,000
6%

Developed International
$45,000
18%

Emerging Markets
$10,000
4%

Corporate Bonds
$100,000
40%

Profile of Leon and Sharon Washington

Leon Washington, 50, and his wife, Sharon, 45, plan to retire in 15 years. Leon works for an architectural firm while Sharon works in human resources. Their daughter Grace, 23, a recent college graduate, is now working and living on her own.

Income Needs

The Washingtons' current combined income is $125,000. They have put away enough funds to pay their bills for a period of nine months should their income stream be disrupted. Now that Grace is independent, they intend to focus on building their nest egg and adding at least $15,000 per year to their investment account. Except in the event of an emergency, they do not anticipate taking any withdrawals from the portfolio for a minimum of 15 years.

Investment Sentiment

Leon and Sharon have always focused on their finances, kept to a budget, and put aside whatever they could for retirement. They understand the marketplace, volatility, and the tradeoffs between risk and reward, and they are willing to take some risk to build their nest egg in a more robust fashion.

Investment Objective

The Washingtons' goal is to enjoy a comfortable retirement lifestyle. They aren't focused on leaving Grace a large legacy but rather on her being self-supporting and independent.

Recommendation

The Washingtons are in a typical Baby Boomer situation. Concentrating on building their home, creating their lifestyle, and educating their offspring, they put savings on the back burner. Not until they became empty-nesters did they have the ability to start putting away meaningful money for their own future. To catch up, they have to make their money work hard without taking undue risk. Rather than swinging for the fences, they should focus on not striking out. They do not need a fixed income allocation in their portfolio to produce current spendable income, but a strong allocation to that sector will dampen the volatility of their slightly more aggressive equity allocations.

Prototypical Aggressive Allocation

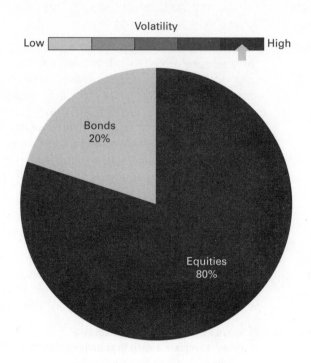

Portfolio Objective

Emphasis on long-term capital appreciation

Portfolio Characteristics

Significant volatility
Relatively low current income
Higher long-term growth potential
Higher potential inflation protection

Allocation Considerations

An overweight to equities to provide the opportunity for significant capital appreciation

The equity allocation should:

- Be well-diversified to avoid concentration risk from a specific asset class
- Be positioned to participate in worldwide growth opportunities

The bond allocation can:

- Be used to dampen some portfolio volatility
- Provide moderate current income
- Provide a source of funds in lieu of potentially having to sell equities at inopportune times

Investor Profile

Someone who:

- Prefers growth over stability
- Has a high tolerance for volatility
- Doesn't rely on a steady stream of portfolio withdrawals to support lifestyle
- Has capital that can remain invested over long-term market cycles

Suggested Aggressive Allocation

Clients: "Fred and Helen Lee"

Portfolio Size: $45,000

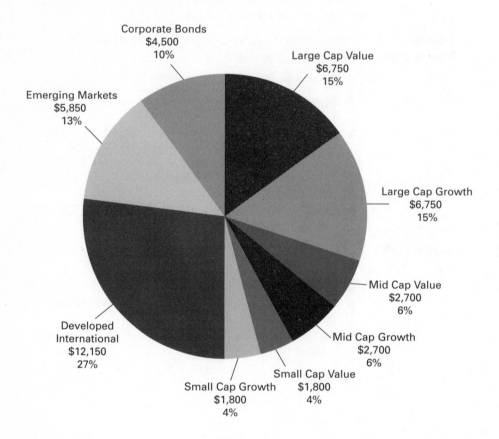

Profile of Fred and Helen Lee

Fred Lee, 29, and his wife, Helen, 27, were recently married and have purchased their first home. Fred is a civil engineer and Helen works for a marketing company. Their combined income is $80,000. They are planning to have children at some point.

Income Needs

Fred and Helen are just beginning their careers. All of their investable capital is tied up in their respective 401(k) employer accounts, to which both have directed 10 percent of their incomes be deposited.

Investment Sentiment

The Lees' investment sentiment in a nutshell: "No one likes to lose money." Since they don't anticipate touching their retirement money for decades, they pay no attention to it.

Investment Objective

Fred and Helen are currently focused on funding their future selves. Their primary objective, before the needs of a growing family reduce their ability to save, is to make sure they set aside a piece of what they make today to help pay for their future retirement.

Recommendation

The Lees have a very long time horizon. They anticipate contributing as much as possible annually to their 401(k) accounts and won't begin making withdrawals for 30 years. There is only a negligible risk that a portfolio heavily weighted in equities won't produce a solid return over such a long time. Since they don't keep track of what's happening in their 401(k)—though they should—they don't react to volatility. In any case, volatility should not derail their very long-term plans.

Suggested Aggressive Allocation

Client: "Abe Cohen"

Portfolio Size: $5,000,000

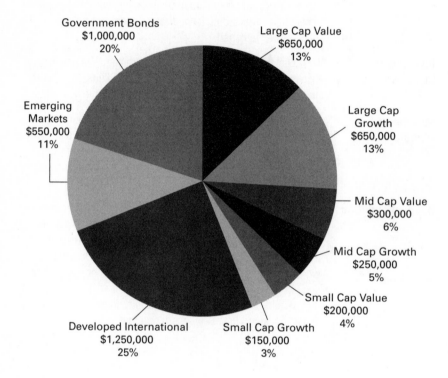

Profile of Abe Cohen

Abe Cohen, 73, retired five years ago from a senior executive position at a major manufacturing company. A widower for a decade, he likes to spend a lot of time with his two sons, Kevin, 43, and Leonard, 40, and their families.

Income Needs

Abe has been and will always be a saver. Despite the wealth he has amassed, he lives very modestly. His sons tease that he has the first nickel he ever made. To augment the income he receives from his pension and Social Security, Abe withdraws only $50,000 per year from his portfolio— a 1 percent withdrawal rate—and most of it goes toward gifts for his grandchildren. He certainly could spend more but he sees no reason to do so.

Investment Sentiment

Abe has never tolerated market volatility very well. He likes to see his accounts grow steadily and hates when the values on his statements go down. As a result, he has only modest investments in equities and keeps most of his assets in high-quality municipal bonds. But current events have left Abe worried about the threat that inflation posses to his legacy. Recognizing that he will never spend all of his money, he now wants to keep as much of its future buying power intact as possible to take care of future generations.

Investment Objective

To allocate enough capital to provide the relatively modest amount of money he needs to withdraw annually and position the balance to grow for his children's and grandchildren's benefit.

Recommendation

Abe's age and personal needs do not make him an obvious candidate for a more aggressive portfolio. His earning years are behind him, and getting strong returns won't enhance his lifestyle. But he has determined that his money should now be invested in accordance with his sons' time horizon—25 to 35 years. Given his life expectancy, he doesn't feel that being aggressive will jeopardize his ability to withdraw money from his portfolio sufficient enough to support his lifestyle. He is focused on growing his assets to combat the effects of inflation, which he fears will erode the legacy he long expected to leave his children and grandchildren.

Key Takeaways

■ **Decide what you believe in.** If you're looking for returns that emulate the returns produced by the market as a whole, then a passive investing style (buying index funds) will suit your needs. If, on the other hand, your investment philosophy is that returns can be enhanced by managers who look for opportunities and keep you out of places you don't want to be, then you should choose active management.

■ **Understand the different risks that equity categories imply.** The rule of thumb is that conservative investors lean toward "value" stocks, which are generally considered bargains—either because a company is considered stodgy though well established or perhaps because a current problem has put a company (and even a sector) in disfavor. "Growth" stocks—from companies that are creating buzz and expanding—are more likely to be favored by more aggressive investors. But companies can shift between categories.

■ **Choose your shopping style.** You may decide to invest in mutual funds, in which case you add your money to a pool and managers make the buy and sell decisions. Your only decision is whether to buy the fund. Exchange-traded funds share many characteristics of mutual funds, though they are generally passive investments. Another option is to work with a broker to construct a portfolio just for you, or, if you have enough capital, you can consider a separately managed account.

■ **Don't confuse your investment temperament with your investment objectives**. Your personal sentiments may be conservative, but that doesn't mean that you should never be exposed to volatility. While you have to be comfortable with your plan to stick with it, a well-thought-out plan should be guided by your goals rather than your personality.

9

Employ Defensive Moves

AS YOU'VE SEEN, you might have given up control of your nest egg in ways you didn't even realize. But you can reclaim it: by embracing asset allocation as your philosophy, establishing your investment principles, and devising a plan that suits your goals.

Once you've put everything into place, you want to keep it safe. Take measures to protect your nest egg from being shattered by a catastrophic event or depleted too quickly in your retirement years.

Offload Your Risk

Certain life events can siphon off enough of your assets to derail all your future plans. Rather than take the chance that one will blindside you, you can build a budget item into your current planning that shifts the risk to someone else: Buy "wealth insurance"—coverage to handle foreseeable expenses that might vaporize your resources.

For comprehensive protection, you need several types of insurance: *medical, disability,* and *long-term care* insurance to cover the cost of health expenses and replace lost income; *property insurance* to provide funds to repair or replace your tangible assets, and *casualty/liability insurance* to protect you against claims for losses caused by injury to others or damage to the property of others.

Medical Insurance

If you presently have medical coverage through your job, your employer did the homework and made the decisions for you. But once you leave the workforce, everything is in your hands. You may not have anticipated the time it takes to find a plan that meets your specific needs along with your financial concerns. And you will probably be floored to discover how substantial a budget item this can be.

There's a lot to consider: Will you have to cover dependents? How much preventive care will be included? To what extent, if any, will hearing, dental, or vision costs be covered? What kind of coverage do you want in the event of injury or the need for surgery? How much freedom do you want in being able to choose your doctors? There is a tremendous—even overwhelming—amount of information available online and from other resources. But the importance of getting your medical health insurance right cannot be overstated.

Even when you're eligible for Medicare, you don't enter a worry-free zone. Though most people are covered for hospital insurance, you will be charged monthly for medical insurance, and the charge goes up as you pass certain income thresholds. Most likely, you will also want to consider a private "Medigap" plan—a supplement meant to fill in the many areas where coverage isn't complete—as well as a plan for drug coverage.

There are specific federal and state guidelines for the various plans you will be offered, but not all insurance companies offer every plan, and costs for the plans vary from insurance company to insurance company.

How the health care reforms signed into law in the spring of 2010 will affect you may not be entirely clear for some time to come. For the latest information check the web site www.healthreform.gov. The current information on Medicare guidelines and options is available from the web site www.medicare.gov.

When you add the cost of all the coverage, it can run into many thousands of dollars, and even then your medical costs aren't all met (because of copayments and excluded items). But many of the costs of a catastrophic illness will probably be covered.

Disability Insurance

If you are a pre-retiree who is still in the workforce your employment benefits package may include disability insurance that is meant to protect you and your dependents against loss of income. Even so, you may discover that there are so many exclusions in the generic package that you might need supplemental coverage. If you're self-employed, disability insurance is imperative.

Contrary to the general assumption, most disabilities aren't the result of accidents but are the side effects of illnesses such as heart disease and cancer. The American Council of Life Insurers says that one-third of all Americans aged 35 to 65 will become disabled, and one in seven will be disabled for more than five years.

It's critical to go over the specifics of an existing or proposed policy very carefully—not just the amount of the benefit, the waiting period, and the length of benefit coverage but also other factors such as benefits for partial and recurrent disabilities, and cost of living adjustments.

Pay close attention to the details—how "disability" is defined, on what basis "replacement income" is calculated, whether bonuses are insured, and all the other fine print—to be sure that your coverage will do what you expect. To be absolutely certain, you should have it reviewed by an expert.

Long-Term Care Insurance

Long-term care insurance is a topic that inspires a lot of pushback. Most people erroneously assume that they'll need long-term care only for an event so devastating that they'll be in a vegetative state. So they find some way to rationalize not buying this protection.

This won't happen to me, they say. Or they cite the medical history of parents who were struck down suddenly but suffered no extended illnesses—ignoring the fact that people today may live a long time with diseases that were once brief and terminal.

Others rely on the government to step in, but while some long-term care may be available, it's only for people in the lowest income groups. Yet another rationale—*My kids will take care of me*—is increasingly unlikely in a world where the nuclear family is scattered and "the kids" have other obligations and may be unequal to the task. And some people just say, *I'll take my chances.* You'd better be completely certain you can afford to leave such a potential liability on your balance sheet.

Today, long-term care insurance is sought even by people with substantial wealth. A decade or two ago, they might have self-insured, but now insurance specialists say that more people prefer to shift the risk to an insurer. That's because in the past, long-term care insurance was typically used to cover an end-of-life stay in a nursing home that was likely to last just three or four years. Due to advances in medical care, heart disease, cancer, and other conditions are now treated as long-term, chronic illnesses.

A patient may at first get assistance from a family member, and then home care might be necessary. That might be followed by assisted living and, eventually, a relatively short nursing home or hospice stay. Such a long process can be a tremendous drain on anyone's assets. The way to protect them is with long-term care insurance.

What you are buying with long-term care insurance is a pool of money that comes from someone else's balance sheet. The contract and the benefits you select determine how it gets used up. If the cost per day is less than the amount for which you're insured, the benefits will continue until the total amount of insurance is depleted. More expensive policies insure you for an indefinite period.

An extreme situation I'm aware of probably makes this case most poignantly. A healthy, 67-year-old woman took out a long-term care policy just to be prudent. She had paid only one semiannual premium when she suffered a debilitating stroke. Her insurance delivered what she had bought: protection against the unexpected. She lived another eight years without paying one additional cent for care that would otherwise have cost her (or her family) close to $300 a day, or more than $850,000.

Aside from the amount and length of coverage, you have to decide whether you want inflation protection and how long an elimination period you want—that is, how long you're willing to cover expenses out of your own pocket before the insurance begins. Extending the waiting period will reduce your premiums.

Compare at least two or three products, check the company history in terms of rate increases (sometimes you can lock in your initial premium), look at the company's ratings, and make sure you have a waiver of premium once your policy is activated. Ask for details about all the latest options—for example, a shared husband/wife policy (where the coverage can be extended to either, depending on needs) and a new private/public partnership program that offers a policy that can protect a specific amount of assets for inheritance purposes.

It's prudent to start considering long-term care insurance in your early 50s, before you're likely to have the kind of physical problems that will exclude you from coverage or disqualify you from preferred rates. In any case, at that age you may be able to lock in rates low enough so that even if you pay for many years, you're still ahead.

Life Insurance

I think everyone understands the need for life insurance as income replacement in the event that the family breadwinner passes away. But it's also important to consider it in the context of offloading risk.

As I've said, I firmly believe that your obligation to a spouse supersedes all others, and your planning should be calculated to take both of you—together or individually—to the finish line. Rather than take the chance that out-pocket-costs for a serious health problem may devastate your financial plans, you can rely on the proceeds of life insurance to replenish resources for the benefit of a surviving spouse and anyone else whom you intend to protect with your nest egg.

Life insurance can also provide cash to cover estate taxes. While a surviving spouse is exempted from inheritance tax obligations, other heirs are not. Having insurance proceeds to pay taxes also protects your heirs from being forced to sell illiquid assets at inappropriate times (or in times when there is a limited market for them). Discuss with an advisor what kind of life insurance will cover such a situation and how to ensure that the proceeds aren't taxable.

Property/Casualty and Liability Insurance

Property/casualty and liability coverage insure your physical possessions (your home, car, boat, jewelry, furniture and art) against loss and damage due to perils like fire, wind, lightning and vandalism, and they protect you from liability for losses caused by injury to other people or damage to their property.

Read such policies closely to see what is excluded. You may realize that you need separate earthquake insurance if you live in a region where they're a threat. But you might not recognize that you need flood insurance even if you live in Arizona. Whether the flood is due to natural causes or a burst pipe, coverage for the damage it creates is not standard in a homeowner's policy.

And though you can't take a car off a lot without an insurance certificate, there is no such requirement when you buy a powerboat, jet skis, a moped, or a motorcycle. This is another example of a liability that your existing policies may not cover.

Umbrella Liability Insurance

This insurance is so named because it acts as a protective cover on your auto and homeowner's liability insurance by giving you extra protection. Some people opt out of this additional coverage because they mistakenly believe that if they are sued—due to a major traffic accident, a serious slip and fall someone sustains on their property, or one of their trees crashing through a neighbor's roof—having a substantial amount of coverage makes them a bigger target.

In fact, while the name of your company has to be revealed in the event of a lawsuit, the amount of your protection does not. And if you're in a situation where you do need it, I can assure you that the bigger the umbrella, the more comfortable you'll be.

I know of a case where a youngster was badly burned because of a freak accident at a backyard barbecue. The child's family sued the host and won a large settlement. Because the host didn't have enough insurance, he was financially ruined. Sure, this is a rare and unlikely event, but all lawsuits are the result of rare and unlikely events.

Be sure to look under the covers if you find a "bargain" policy. The rates may be low because you have insufficient personal injury coverage (for harm to yourself) or your policy may delay or disallow renewal of your liability coverage if someone is successful in suing you.

Manage Your Decumulation

All the discipline and effort you applied to reclaiming your nest egg is meant to give you the comfort of knowing that you have provided for your future self. So your responsibility as a wealth manager can't end with accumulation. You also have to manage the process of tapping into and living off your assets—a process best described as *decumulation*.

In fact, you have to plan decumulation even more carefully than you planned accumulation, because every withdrawal makes your total portfolio increasingly vulnerable.

In the years when you're building your assets, despite the inevitable periods of volatility, your nest egg increases because you're making ongoing contributions and taking no withdrawals and because, historically, investments generally grow bigger over time.

Still, volatility might have had some negative effect. The swings of the market might have led you to make some of the irrational, emotional, and damaging decisions that I've described. And though your assets may have grown, the stumbles and recoveries caused by volatility may have kept some of that growth in check.

Consider: If a $10,000 investment goes down 10 percent, to $9,000, it has to come back 11 percent before you to make any forward progress. If it goes down 25 percent, to $7,500, it has to grow by more than 33⅓ percent. And if it goes down 50 percent, to $5,000, it has to go up over 100 percent for you to return to your starting point!

What's more, once you're in decumulation mode, the downward movement of the market delivers a double whammy. Your portfolio has to recover not just from the effects of the slump but also from the fact that your withdrawal has reduced the amount of money available to rebound.

That's why managing your rate of withdrawal during down periods is especially critical. While I've made the point numerous times that you shouldn't allow volatility to affect your decision making while you're accumulating money, at this point in your money management career, you absolutely cannot ignore it.

Customize Your Strategy

Not only does decumulation have to be managed very carefully, but also it's got to be customized for your own particular situation since there are so many elements to consider.

Some of them are unpredictable factors that are related to the overall economic environment. These include the rate of inflation, changes in income tax rates, and current market conditions.

Other factors relate to your specific circumstances:

■ What are your total resources?

■ What's the duration of your planned retirement?

■ What are your sources of income other than your portfolio— wages, Social Security, pension, real estate investments, trusts—and how reliable and predictable are they?

■ Do you anticipate any inheritance?

■ What is your health situation and what is your life expectancy?

■ What size withdrawals from your portfolio are necessary to maintain your lifestyle?

■ How often do you plan to make withdrawals?

■ Do you have any obligation (or potential obligation) to take care of family members?

There's no universal template to help you with decumulation. Still, I can offer some guidelines to help you create your policy. To begin with, based on the longevity projections mentioned in Chapter 1, you know that if your expectation is to retire at 65, your financial planning should be long-term—30 years or more.

A sustainable rate of withdrawal should be based on percentages, not dollars. A good rate to start with is 4 percent. The reason why I recommend that rate is graphically explained in Figure 9.1.

You'll see that if your portfolio consists of 50 percent stocks, and if at age 65 you start withdrawing at the rate of 3 percent a year

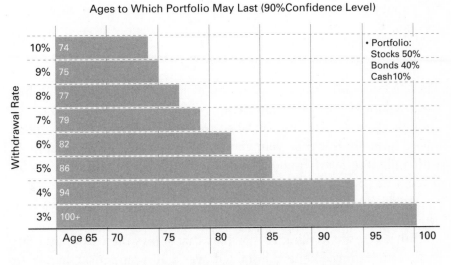

Ages to Which Portfolio May Last (90%Confidence Level)

Figure 9.1 High Withdrawal Will Quickly Deplete Assets

Source: © 2010 Morningstar. All rights reserved. 3/1/2010.

IMPORTANT: Projections generated by Morningstar regarding the likelihood of various investment outcomes are hypothetical in nature, do not reflect actual investment results, and are not guarantees of future results. Results may vary over time and with each simulation. This chart is for illustrative purposes only and not indicative of any investment. An investment cannot be made directly in an index.

and increase your withdrawals annually at the historic inflation-adjusted rate (3.1 percent), you should have a 90 percent certainty that your assets will last until you reach age 100.

Now, while it's logical to assume that if your rate of return exceeds your withdrawal rate, your portfolio should last forever, that ignores the cumulative effect of taxes and inflation on the real growth of buying power that you need to maintain your lifestyle.

So, based on this chart, if you have a $500,000 portfolio, you should be able to start with a $15,000 withdrawal (a 3 percent rate) and increase your annual withdrawals by 3.1 percent without fear that the well will run dry. But if you change the rate just a bit—to $20,000 (a 4 percent rate) or $25,000 (5 percent)—the effect is considerable.

The bigger your withdrawals, the shorter the period your assets will last. If you withdraw at a rate of 4 percent starting at age 65, it's likely your assets will last until you're 94, but if you're pulling out the money at a rate of 10 percent, you'll run out in just nine years, by age 74.

Asset Mix Affects Withdrawals

There's a reason why the illustration in Figure 9.1 assumes that half the investment portfolio is invested in stocks. Most people don't have enough assets to live on bond-like returns, particularly in a climate where rates are low. For your money to appreciate and to keep pace with inflation, you should consider maintaining 40 percent to 50 percent of your investments in well-diversified equities.

Again, an illustration makes this easier to understand. Take a look at Figure 9.2.

What you are looking at is a chart that shows the withdrawal rate that an investor could have sustained over a 30-year period, had he or she retired in any year starting from 1926 to 1979.

Look first at the three horizontal lines, each of which represents a different portfolio mix. In the top line, the equity portion represents 75 percent; in the middle it's 50 percent; and, in the lowest line, 25 percent. As you'll see from the relative and consistent movement

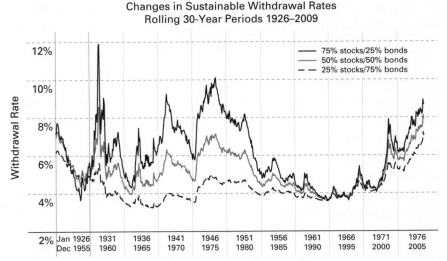

Figure 9.2 How Asset Mix Affects Withdrawal Rates

Source: © 2010 Morningstar. All rights reserved. 3/1/2010.

of the lines, the larger the equity portion in your retirement portfolio, the higher the amounts you would have been able to withdraw.

The benefit of being very conservative by holding mostly bonds is having a lot of predictability. For the entire period, the portfolio containing 75 percent bonds and only 25 percent equities allowed a rate of withdrawal without significant fluctuation. But having so little exposure to equities limits growth and could constrain your ability to cover your cost of living, particularly when you factor in inflation.

This chart also makes it clear that when you retire can have as much impact on your future lifestyle as the size of your nest egg. If you retired at a propitious time, you could consistently have withdrawn a large sum, but retiring into the teeth of a bad market can have a major negative effect.

As we can see with the benefit of hindsight, people who retired in 1931, just before the market began its trajectory out of the Depression, would have been able to withdraw nearly 12 percent per year over the next 30 years.

In contrast, those who retired in the mid-1960s, when the market for the next 20 years remained virtually flat, would have preserved their portfolios only by keeping the withdrawal rate to under 4 percent over a 30-year period.

Then the situation reversed itself again. Someone who turned in his or her office keys in 1978 would have lucked into the warm embrace of a 30-year bull market that would have permitted an 8 percent rate of withdrawal.

In addition to the increased likelihood of longevity risk, weighing on today's retirees and prospective retirees is the fact that since 2000, we have been in a sideways market like that of the 1970s. Such a lack of momentum has raised concerns about careful withdrawal management. Every market dip has the potential for a dramatic effect on their lifestyles.

The likelihood is that the market will break out of that low-growth pattern at some point and the 30-year withdrawal rate for people who retired in 2000 and afterward will have the ability to move higher than 4 percent, but until 2030, when we can look back, we won't know for sure.

Since a safe rate of withdrawal can only be determined in hindsight, the only prudent approach is to be as cautious as possible in the early years of retirement and make adjustments as time goes on.

Is Your Lifestyle Sustainable?

I meet many people for the first time after they've undergone a major life event such as the sale of a business, receipt of an inheritance, a divorce, or widowhood. Many other clients seek advice when they start thinking about retirement. Once they have recognized the complexity of the planning, they decide to seek counsel from people who have helped others go through this process and learned from those experiences. After all, you can only be good at planning for 100 percent of what you can anticipate. What you really need is help dealing with things you didn't anticipate, because those are stumbling blocks that can bring you down.

What the people planning retirement have on their minds usually boils down to one key question: *How much can I withdraw from my nest egg each year?*

"I don't know," I say. "How much does it cost to be you?"

Confronting that question often creates an epiphany for my clients. While people may have a pretty good idea of how much money they have, it's far less likely that they know what it really costs to sustain them. Finding the answer is our starting point. The process of finding the answer causes my clients to come to grips with the fact that they need to have a plan, and sets them on the path of dealing with all the issues I've covered in this book.

Calculating the number of dollars you're living on and determining whether your lifestyle is sustainable is the wakeup call for everyone. That's the cold bucket of water.

The sooner you start this process the better, because time will be on your side. You not only have years to let the nest egg grow but also time to make any necessary adjustments to a standard of living that you can finance.

For some people, no adjustments will be necessary. Others, once they start calculating what it costs to be them, may come around to a different way of thinking about retirement: asking not how much can they take out, but (especially in the beginning years), how *little* they can comfortably live on.

If in retirement you can meet your income needs by withdrawing less than 3 percent annually from your portfolio, consider yourself very fortunate. Otherwise, figure out how you're going to live on a starting withdrawal rate that shouldn't exceed 4 percent of your portfolio.

Do you have to stay there? It depends. Just as an annual physical checkup is essential, so is an annual financial checkup. And just as your M.D. begins to focus on different physical checkpoints as you age, once you're in the decumulation years, the focus of your financial concerns changes as well.

You have to see how current events are affecting your portfolio's longevity, and you have to take a look at whether your withdrawal rate is still in what I call the "retirement safety zone."

In a rising market, as your portfolio grows, so does the dollar amount of your 4 percent withdrawal, providing you with inflation protection and more cash to spend. But when the market goes down, if you're expecting to withdraw a particular dollar amount, that amount may represent 5 percent, 6 percent, even 7 percent of a diminished portfolio.

It's easier to understand this when you see it in terms of numbers. If you have a $500,000 portfolio, and you're planning to withdraw at the rate of 4 percent, you're counting on $20,000.

If the market has done well, and you now have a portfolio of $600,000, withdrawing 4 percent for the following year will reap you $24,000. But if the portfolio has gone down to $400,000, 4 percent is only $16,000. Taking out $20,000 will represent a 5 percent withdrawal rate.

In most cases, that's okay—temporarily.

Just as I tell my clients not to think the sky is falling whenever volatility drives the market down during the accumulation years, I urge them not to overreact to short-term dips in the decumulation years. If your withdrawal goes up to 5 percent for a single year, you don't need to lose sleep.

But if the market remains flat or continues downward, and it appears your portfolio will not rise enough to bring your withdrawal rate back to 4 percent, you're moving out of the safety zone. A withdrawal rate of 5 percent two years in a row is a yellow flag—meaning proceed with caution.

Continuing at that rate can wreak havoc on your long-term goals, as you saw back in Figure 9.1, and your nest egg is unlikely to give you support for the necessary number of years. You'll have to look at your lifestyle decisions and figure out a way to get back below 5 percent so that your portfolio can refuel itself in a rebound.

That's why I started out by saying that your withdrawal rate has to be based on percentages, not dollar amounts. Though much about the movement of the markets is unpredictable, you *can* be certain that taking out 4 percent of your assets will not yield the same number of dollars every year. If you mentally lock yourself into a lifestyle based on a specific amount, you set yourself up for the possibility of outliving your money.

I help my clients work through their calculations annually. Having an advisor work with you helps keep things unemotional. But if you're doing your planning on your own, I strongly recommend that you set down your withdrawal policy in writing, and don't allow yourself to deviate from your guidelines.

Without having someone act as your enforcer or without committing to a written policy of your own, you're vulnerable to veering way off course. Faced with a "pay cut" in your withdrawal rate, it's easy to say, *I'll deal with it next year*, and just take out the dollar amount you're used to. That's why you need to deal with that second-year 5 percent warning signal and, if need be, get a real handle on how much of a cut you must take.

At the other end of the spectrum, after a good year, in the rosy afterglow of a huge market rise, you may be tempted to give yourself too big a raise. Though it's rash to harvest windfalls until you're quite elderly, people do it all the time. But you should put a lid on your raises, and not consider withdrawing more than 6 percent or 7 percent.

In any event, put a mechanism in your life that will emulate the discipline of working with a planner. Doing a recalculation on an annual basis to make sure you're in the safety zone can greatly enhance the longevity of your nest egg.

Over time, as things change—if the market has done very well; if your needs decrease (you've paid off your mortgage, you're traveling less, you've had a windfall inheritance or life insurance payouts); or even if all the factors remained constant and your portfolio has maintained itself—it's likely you'll want to reanalyze your situation. You might do the same as your life expectancy changes. If you have made other arrangements for your legacy concerns, you may not worry about spending down your principal at some point you may reach an age where ignoring the guidelines may not really matter because you'll have sufficient funds to get you to your goal line no matter what the market is doing.

Withdrawal Order Matters

Once you've decided on the initial rate, you have to decide from which accounts to take your withdrawals.

Depending on the size and complexity of your estate, it may make sense to spend down in a particular order that might take precedence over the plan I'm describing here. Discuss those issues with your accountant, estate attorney, or advisor. But to maximize what you can get out of your nest egg, most people will probably benefit from the following guidelines.

If you ignore them, the consequences won't necessarily knock a hole in your retirement planning; but taking advantage of them can make a lifestyle difference by leaving substantially more of your dollars in your own pocket rather than Uncle Sam's. The order of withdrawal is significant primarily because of tax considerations. Otherwise, it wouldn't matter where you take the first money from: your regular portfolio, your IRA or 401(k), or your Roth IRA or Roth 401(k).

Because they're not thinking about the tax consequences, a lot of people make the mistake of making their first retirement withdrawals from the IRA or 401(k) bucket, because they have always seen this as separate, "extra" money rather than as an integrated part of their assets. But the prime benefit of a 401(k) or IRA is that it allows the money you put aside to grow on a tax-free or tax-deferred basis.

The first money you pull out should instead come from taxable accounts. You have to start by considering the cost basis—that is, what you originally paid—for all of the securities in your portfolio. Then, first sell the securities for which your cost basis is high relative to the current market price—the securities that are now worth less than or about the same as what you paid. If you take a loss on the sale, you can use it to offset the tax consequences of future gains; and if your gains are very modest, your tax obligations will be small as well. Remember, taxes are a part of lifestyle.

After you sell the securities with the highest cost basis, go down the chain. The low-basis securities—the ones for which you paid the least relative to current market value—should go last, because of the relatively larger tax bill their sale will incur.

Of course, while you're keeping one eye on where you're withdrawing from, you have to keep the other on ensuring that withdrawals don't cause over- or underconcentration in any one area. You have to remain properly diversified. As I've said before, in a different context, you don't want the tax tail to wag the dog.

The only factor that might cause you to change your strategy is if you anticipate that there will be a substantial increase in the capital gains tax rate, which is the preferential tax treatment on the sale of securities you've held for over a year. In that case, you might want to reverse the procedure and sell your low-basis securities first, before the tax increase takes effect.

Only after you've dealt with your other accounts should you turn your attention to your tax-deferred accounts, like traditional 401(k)s and IRAs. That's because you should let the money in tax-deferred accounts grow as long as possible. Also, you have to pay income tax on any withdrawals from these accounts, since no money was taxed going in. (Once you reach age 70½ you are obliged to take out a minimal mandated percentage of these accounts, and you'll net only what is left after the tax is deducted.)

Last of all, pull out money from tax-free investments, like Roth 401(k)s or Roth IRAs. These funds were taxed when they were deposited, so all investment return is never taxed and all withdrawals are free of any additional taxes whatsoever. Roth accounts are your highest-octane pool of money since they are not burdened by income taxation.

You should leave money in Roths undisturbed as long as possible, since this tax-free accumulation over time can have a material impact on wealth accumulation. Another significant benefit of a Roth is that unlike regular IRAs and 401(k)s there are no required minimum distributions, thus allowing many more years of tax-free accumulation.

Although the Roth assets are subject to certain distribution rules, their benefits can be passed on to the beneficiaries of your estate.

Addressing decumulation issues enhances everything your nest egg can do for you. It pays to seek out advice and make sure you're doing decumulation right.

To keep your nest egg from catastrophe and erosion you need the advice of experts. But in your capacity as your own wealth manager, you may have other reasons to seek professional counsel.

Key Takeaways

- **Buy wealth insurance.** Your well-conceived plan can unravel due to a catastrophic event, such as a natural disaster that affects your home, a medical emergency, or an accident for which the liability is yours. The insurance industry was founded to cover such possibilities. Explore and buy the appropriate insurance so that you downsize your risk to a relatively minor annual budget item rather than leave yourself open to an event that can rob you of your entire nest egg.
- **Be disciplined about your spending.** There isn't much wiggle room in making your decumulation calculations. You have to be realistic and accurate in considering your budget, factoring in not only your present lifestyle needs but allowing for major future expenses (both the ones you can predict and the ones you can't). Get your projected budget and projected income in alignment, and monitor those numbers on an ongoing basis.
- **Start slowly.** The rate of withdrawal is the most important factor in determining how long your nest egg will last, and a difference of only one or two percentage points can be critical. By setting your initial withdrawal rate to a realistic minimum, you become accustomed to living within boundaries and you allow your nest egg a maximum opportunity to sustain itself.
- **Don't ignore volatility.** In the accumulating years, the ability to remain unswayed by volatility is essential in sticking with your plan. But in your decumulation years, you have to be attentive and responsive to it. A plunge in the market can move your rate of withdrawal outside the safety zone. That may be acceptable for a single year, but when it happens two years in a row, you need to begin to take corrective action.

■ **Consider the tax implications before you make withdrawals.** Most of your life, you tried to keep Uncle Sam from being your partner, and you still don't want to give him more than is necessary. That's why you have to plan the order in which you will withdraw retirement money, drawing it first from accounts where it will trigger the lowest tax bill. However, when you're making your sell decisions, don't lose sight of the need to maintain a well-diversified portfolio.

10

Take the Helm

THE SPECIFIC RETURN YOU get on your money can be far less important in getting you to the finish line than dealing with the big issues that I have covered: getting perspective on what shapes your decisions, finding an investment strategy, coming up with a holistic plan, and then addressing budgeting, asset management, and cash flow.

All these concerns, layered on one another, represent a huge amount of responsibility and great potential for a misstep. What you don't know may not kill you, but it can certainly cause you serious harm.

In considering all that is involved, you have to make a decision about what you will handle on your own and when you'll seek assistance. Being self-reliant means taking ultimate responsibility, but you don't have to go it alone.

Addressing Preservation Issues

A lot of people look first to their accountant as a collaborator. But you can't assume that your accountant has a good picture of your financial situation simply because he or she does your taxes. And not all accountants are able or willing to take on a role beyond tax preparer. A client told me, in fact, that she phoned her accountant to ask why in a year when virtually all her friends were refinancing to lower their mortgage rates, he had not suggested she do the same. "I'm not your financial planner," he said.

At least once a year, at tax time, as you sift through your brokerage account statements, 1099s, and your lists of tax deductions, you may come up with a lot of questions. *Should I be refinancing my mortgage? When I'm eligible, should I take Social Security as soon as possible or defer it? Should I be selling or swapping any securities for tax reasons? Are there any assets I should be transferring to my children?*

Your life insurance coverage should also be reviewed. In the past, life insurance was rarely recommended as a savings/investment vehicle. Financial planners advised forgoing expensive whole life polices in favor of cheap term insurance and applying the savings to your investment pool. But today, because of their tax benefits, whole life and other policies that have savings and investment components make financial sense in certain situations.

Doing your taxes may trigger your questions and concerns, but you'll get short shrift if you attempt to get your answers during tax preparation season. Wait until you can have a more leisurely discussion of taxation and preservation issues with an accountant who's qualified to serve as your planner; or seek out a planner who is knowledgeable about taxes.

Handling Money Management

In a 2008 AARP survey, men and women who had already retired, or were about to be, were asked if they knew how to convert assets into a stream of income that would last for a lifetime. Less than a fifth of people on the verge of retirement said they were very comfortable doing so, and only about a quarter of those who were already retired could say the same.

Still, many people choose to go it on their own. In some cases, the goal is to save on fees and commissions. Others decide to act independently because they feel they've been let down by the people to whom they gave over management responsibility. That was certainly the case following the financial crisis of 2008. The events of that time led a lot of people to question whether there was any value at all in having a financial advisor. They often took a very narrow view of the role such a person played: *He gets me in and out of the market.* Or, *She does an analysis and gives me a thumbs up or thumbs down.* That's simplistic and wrong.

But that narrow view is yet another reason that people choose to manage their own money: because they think they can. There doesn't seem to be much to it, so why pay someone else to do the job? Certainly there's no shortage of advertising meant to create a false sense of security that do-it-yourself investing is easy.

Some books, financial courses, and trading programs continue to suggest that by inputting the right criteria and parameters you can come up with a magic formula that will guarantee your investment success for a lifetime, totally ignoring the fact that the meltdown of 2008 proved that notion illusory.

You'll find many online and other services that promise to handle your asset allocation issues (and also help reduce your tax obligations, manage your Roth and IRA, and choose the amount and kind of insurance you need). My general take on these is that if it doesn't require skill to input the data—if the assumptions are too simplified—then your answers will be oversimplified as well.

The results you get may be useful, but only as a starting point. Don't be lulled into a false sense of security, believing your issues are being thoroughly addressed. You may be relying on generic answers that can be misleading, potentially costly, and possibly disastrous. You can't live with constant worry that your world will come crashing down. That's where the professionals come in. An expert can help weigh assumptions, master facts, answer questions, and frame others.

You want customized attention when you decorate your house or plan a wedding. You demand it when you're getting health care. So shouldn't you think twice before you decide to go without it when you're dealing with your finances?

A Matter of Discipline

I believe that people have the capability to do their own money management. But there's a big difference between *having the capability to* be your own money manager and actually *doing it.* Once you personally take on the tasks at the granular level, if you're going to do it right, you'll find there's a lot to be done: researching and keeping track of funds, corporate developments, industries, and overall economic trends. And as I've pointed out, even if you get it right, the responsibility is ongoing.

You need to maintain your plan and tweak it conscientiously, because the one detail you fail to monitor may turn out to be the one that sabotages it. For example, many high-yield junk bond funds boosted returns in 1993 by investing in debt from developing countries like Argentina and Mexico. You wouldn't have been aware of the increased risk you were taking unless you had read the literature very closely and then taken action. Otherwise, you would have sustained major losses.

More and more information is becoming available to non-professionals, and Google is a wonderful resource; but it's not a money manager, any more than Web MD is a doctor. On top of that, investors often overdose themselves on information, causing a condition called "paralysis by analysis." Effective management isn't just a matter of having the information. You need a point of view. You need the ability to distinguish between research material and a sales pitch, which are often the same document. Indecision and confusion do not spell health for an investment portfolio.

Investing can seem deceptively easy because the concepts aren't hard to grasp. But do you have the time, the inclination, and the perseverance to learn and understand all the variables? More important, how do you filter through all of it? How do you put it to use?

To get the answers you need, you have to start with the questions. Framing the questions is the real challenge. If you aren't absolutely certain you're up to the task by yourself, then you should consider hiring a professional to help manage your assets.

Who's in the Control Tower?

You may have been consulting various sources and working with a bunch of ad hoc players in the past. But to cover all the bases as you go forward, you will most likely reach out to a number of professionals—an asset manager, an accountant, a lawyer, an insurance specialist.

And a team needs a leader. There has to be someone sitting in the control tower to make sure you have an integrated plan. Will you cast yourself in that role? Northern Trust surveyed 1,312 millionaire clients in 2005. Asked to name their financial planner, 45 percent said, "Myself." That may not be the best choice. You don't have the kind of unemotional and objective perspective that a professional can bring to your situation.

Maybe, as I've suggested, your accountant has the experience and the vision to fill the position. Or, if you currently have a money manager and your asset allocation is working, you might use that person, provided he or she has the necessary all-around skills and is sanctioned to take on the job. (An employee of a brokerage firm may not be permitted to work in that capacity.)

But whomever you choose as your overall financial advisor should be qualified to take an all-encompassing, impartial view and to make sure all your financial plans are in line with your specific needs, goals, and aspirations. In my utopian vision, people should be just as incredulous on hearing that you don't have a financial advisor as if you were to say you don't have a doctor or a dentist.

The right person should be able to give you not only counsel and perspective but also foresight—the ability to pick up on anything important that's not on your radar screen now and to look ahead a decade or two and think about what might hurt you in the future. Having a good planner lead your team should mean never having to say, "I didn't think of that."

That person should know all the details of your finances because he or she made the effort to pull them out of you. In fact, if you're not asked a bunch of probing questions, you aren't working with the right person. If the only questions your advisor asks are the ones you can readily answer, he or she is not probing deeply enough.

Your advisor needs to know even about decisions you may be reluctant to share: that you're investing in a nephew's restaurant though his odds of success are very low; that you're supporting an adult child who has returned home after a failed marriage and career missteps; that you're hanging onto stock positions that you know are indefensible but don't want to be chastised about.

While there's no harm in keeping up appearances or revealing facts only on a need-to-know basis with your other counselors, you have to be willing to get financially "naked" with your chief planner. The degree of your faith and trust in your planner's motives is as important as his or her technical knowledge. But you can only be vulnerable to people you can trust. You can only get naked with someone you believe won't steal your clothes.

Getting Unbiased Advice

When you're shopping around for an advisor, be careful where you do the looking.

There's an old saying: *Once you choose an advisor, you've chosen your advice.* That is, if you go to a knee surgeon about a problem with your knee, you'll probably be told to have surgery. Similarly, if you seek financial planning from someone who carries the business card of an insurance company, your financial plan will probably be centered around an insurance solution such as an annuity. If that person is from a brokerage firm, chances are you'll rely on stock and mutual fund solutions, and if you're consulting with a banker, your plan will include banking products, such as certificates of deposit.

What's more, if the financial planning is being offered free of charge, it's probably being offered as a loss leader. The goal of the provider of the plan—a bank, an insurance company, or a brokerage house—is to sell you a product.

You want to make sure that your planning advice is not linked to its implementation. Proper planning is goals-based. A plan that's right for you will suggest a number of ways to hit your goals: adjusting your spending habits, buying insurance, setting a target for your investment earnings, and so forth. It will give you options.

In my firm, planning services are separate from our asset management services unless the client specifically asks to merge them. Of course there are benefits to having them integrated, but it's entirely possible for clients to take a plan that we developed and have it implemented elsewhere.

If you decide to choose an independent planner, where do you start? You shouldn't be lulled into a false sense of confidence by someone carrying a passport from alphabet soup land because that isn't necessarily a guarantee of competence or an assurance of experience. Some people earn the letters that they put after their name when they've merely completed an online correspondence course or a weekend training program.

A referral from someone you trust, especially a peer in the same or a related field, is a good place to begin. But the referral is meaningful only if it comes from someone who has direct experience with the work style and track record of the professional you're interviewing.

If there's someone you're considering as your planner, asking for a general reference won't tell you much because it will invariably be favorable. There may be merit, however, in asking for a reference from a client in a situation similar to yours. At least that client might be able to tell you something about how the planner's approach and strategies worked out in a comparable case.

Among the basic and obvious questions to ask:

■ How much time will you spend with me?

■ Will I be dealing with you, or will I be handed off to someone on the team?

■ What breadth and depth of services do you offer (i.e., tax preparation? Asset allocation? Other?)? I How do you integrate the advice?

■ Describe a typical client. Are you giving advice to people in my circumstances on a daily basis? (You don't want to be a small fish in someone's pond, nor do you want to be a whale with large and complex issues with which the person has no experience.)

■ What kind of interaction and input can I expect, and on how regular a basis?

■ How do you charge: hourly, flat fee, or some other arrangement?

Some not-so-obvious questions might also be informative. For example:

■ How long have you lived in the area? (It's helpful for your advisor to be familiar with what local housing is worth, what tax issues arise, and other matters related to the environment in which you're making your plans.)

■ What did you do before you were a financial planner? (You learn a lot about people when they tell you their life stories.)

Whomever you select should be someone whose skills and business practices match your needs. You shouldn't be looking for someone to be either your best buddy or your economics professor.

Compatibility is probably the most important issue of all. If you know you need hand-holding, hire someone who has the time and temperament to do it. If you require a tremendous amount of detail before you make decisions, work with someone who's unlikely to get exasperated when you ask for the fifteenth permutation of any solution.

Keep in mind that you should feel that what the advisor is communicating matches up with what your common sense and your world experience also tell you.

Working Expert to Expert

Many people try on their own to coordinate the efforts of the professionals they work with, relaying the questions and answers back and forth. Once again, this is a benefit to be gained from choosing someone other than yourself as the head planner. I think it's a plus to have the experts confer among themselves under the direction of the leader who's not you but who is intimate with your overall needs and goals.

They can coordinate efforts, come up with recommendations and supply you with the reasoning behind any action steps at the end of their discussions, but doing the initial work expert-to-expert can be more expedient and practical:

■ It's more focused on the goal. When a client is the intermediary, another professional's good idea may encounter some "not invented here" resistance; and rather than seem uncertain or not knowledgeable about a question from another expert, the specialist you're talking to may simply dismiss it. When the client isn't present, you remove ego from the situation and people are more likely to zero in on the issue itself and be more open to other points of view.

■ It saves time and money. A client in a supervisory role may not be as clear on the issues or lingo as the experts and is likely to transmit ideas and information less efficiently than experts talking among themselves. When a professional is asking the questions, there is no time wasted bringing anyone up to speed.

■ It helps ensure that topics are thoroughly addressed. Clients attempting to keep billable hours to a minimum sometimes edit information too tightly. They're concerned that it will cost a lot to get an answer to a question that they may mistakenly believe is tangential.

■ It encourages creative thinking. Tossing around ideas in a group situation often helps people think outside of the box.

■ It's synergistic. Many issues cut across several lines of expertise, and when the information is shared, the client can benefit greatly. As I previously pointed out, clients who are very invested in tax-free bonds may be able to add some higher-yielding corporate bonds without being put in a higher tax bracket. Without input from the accountant, an asset allocation manager may not even be aware that this approach is practical for your situation.

■ It provides a built-in system of checks and balances. An insurance expert working with an accountant and planner is unlikely to recommend insurance that doesn't really suit your needs, and a stockbroker won't risk suggesting a product that would cause eye rolling among the professionals who foresee the pitfalls it might pose.

■ It's less prone to error. In a group environment, the leader (and team members) are quicker and likelier to spot and resolve any inconsistencies. They can look at things side by side to see if they're contradictory. For example, a trust document might assume that your assets are titled in a way that they are not, which in turn would negate your attorney's work. With many eyes looking on, someone is likely to notice if proposed solutions are incompatible or impractical.

The hardest part of every endeavor is not getting the answers, but knowing the questions. Almost all problems arise because there was a question you didn't know enough to ask. That's why a holistic team effort is so helpful; the lawyers will ask different questions than the accountants, who will ask different questions than the insurance people. They'll all introduce you to concepts you weren't aware of and help ensure there are no holes in your plan. Figuring out the right questions will develop the shock absorbers that keep you and the people in your world safe—and is likely to be less costly in the long run.

By putting together a good and sound plan, not only can you protect your own financial future, but also you can go beyond that—to protect the future of the people you love and who depend on you.

Key Takeaways

■ **Be realistic about your need for assistance.** I have no doubt that you can implement all the principles in this book on your own. But having the intellect and information you need may not translate into having the will or time to follow through. Decide whether you're going to make managing your assets part of your responsibilities—not just for the next three months but also on an ongoing basis. If you can't make that commitment, think about working with a professional.

- **Pick your advisors cautiously.** From time to time, to resolve issues that are directly or indirectly related to your financial situation (such as legal, insurance, or accounting matters), you'll need advice from a specialist in the field. Get recommendations from people you trust and, when possible, who are in a situation similar to yours.
- **Bear in mind that quality advice comes at a price.** Customized planning takes time, and you should expect to pay for it. Free advice is often a loss leader, proposed by an advisor who stands to make a commission on the recommended solution, such as an annuity or a particular family of funds. Implementation advice should be independent of planning advice. There should be a variety of implementation alternatives suitable to carry out a sound plan.

Epilogue

AS IS OFTEN THE CASE with people who make a living by selling advice, some members of the financial services industry try to dazzle and confuse by talking in jargon. They haul out the spreadsheets and the formulas, and they start talking about things like correlation coefficients. This is all meant to make them look smart. Even more important, it creates a sense of dependency in the listener. The less you understand, the clearer the message: *I'm the expert, and you're not.*

I take the contrary approach. I want to create a bond of understanding. I want everyone to realize that you don't need college level courses, advanced degrees, or Albert Einstein's brain to understand the principles of managing your money. In this book, I have tried to do just what I do when talking to my clients—demystify everything, make everything accessible, and strip it all down to the very basic concepts.

I've built my career on the assumption that real comfort comes from knowing *why* things are done rather than *how*. I want my clients to realize they can't outsource all responsibility. They have to "own" the information and understand it all thoroughly and well enough to build on it.

I'm very comfortable doing this, and I never worry that educating my clients is going to put me out of business. Understanding the principles is one thing. Putting them into practice is another.

Professionally, I see my responsibilities as helping people discover their needs and then implementing the solutions—making sure my clients' funds are allocated in an appropriate fashion, and then regularly monitoring and reexamining the various aspects of their financial plans to make sure everything is working the way it's supposed to. Yes, it's possible to do it on your own. But most people will not.

The people who entrust me to manage their nest eggs are very successful. They couldn't have amassed their assets if they were dumb, clueless, incompetent, or helpless. They just don't have the time and focus to be on top of all the changing variables in the way that's needed to run their money effectively.

The number one way I help them is by making all the connections clear so they feel empowered to protect and build on what they have spent a lifetime accumulating. I have the same goals for my readers.

I have said that how people think about their money has a lot more to do with whether they'll reach their goals than any investment choice they'll make. I can't drive that message home hard enough. Understanding the reasoning behind decisions is so much more important than understanding the tactics.

You have absolutely no control over the market. What you can control is your own hand on the wheel. But that's only if you recognize what makes you lose control—the head trash you should dump, the media yanking your chains, and the financial services industry that may not be responsive to your particular needs—and why you have to stay focused to reach your goal.

I'm an optimistic guy, and I have plenty of reason to be. History backs me up. Though the stock market has had its downs, when you take the long view, it has climbed steadily upward. So the chances are that you're way closer to reclaiming your nest egg than you think. Once you develop a realistic perception of the lifestyle your assets can support, face the mistakes of the past, and blow the dust off old documents, the benefits are huge. With a plan you believe in and principles to stick to, you can put those pieces together, reclaim your nest egg, and wrap things up.

Your job isn't done until you're sure that the people to whom you're going to pass everything on to know what you've left and where you left it. They, too, have to understand how the pieces fit together and be fully prepared to carry your legacy forward. True comfort comes from taking care of your responsibilities beyond your own finish line and leaving peace and harmony behind.

In this regard, the generation before the Baby Boomers produced poor role models. Think how little you knew about the financial affairs of your parents. Unless finance was the family business, people didn't talk about money. Dad went to work and came home with a paycheck. He protected the family from the details of how the bills were paid and the money was managed.

Over three decades of dealing with people, I've seen that you have to take people into the tent with you to avoid unintended consequences. If they don't know anything about what you're thinking, you jeopardize the chance for peace and harmony and open the door to ambiguity, dissention, and chaos.

If your planning is poor and your instructions are unclear or nonexistent, your heirs won't know what to do with what you've left them. A huge hunk of their legacy may evaporate with inefficiencies and rookie mistakes as they make their way along the investment learning curve.

After the tremors in the market began in 2008, I was consulted by some people who had previously inherited a substantial amount but had no money management experience. The fact that they'd done well in the market run-up in the mid-2000s gave them a lot of false confidence. It's easy to credit your own brains when the bull market is raising all boats. But when the environment became stormy and the market sank 50 percent, they began second-guessing their decisions and realized that they didn't really know as much as they thought.

Among them was a guy who had sold everything in his late father's portfolio. When the market started going down, he had seen danger everywhere, so he fled. He came to me after everything had begun to climb back up. He was sitting on the sidelines with his pile of cash, trying to calculate when to get back in—making the classic beginner's mistake of thinking there's a way to time the market.

After reviewing the statement from his father's account, I realized the dad had done his homework. The portfolio had been so well diversified that the upheaval of the markets wouldn't have undermined the integrity of the allocations over the long term. But because the son was unaware of the built-in shock absorbers, he undid decades of careful thought by bailing out. Soon, he realized what a mistake he had made and how much better off he would have been had he left everything as it was.

This is a perfect cautionary tale, demonstrating why I suggest that my clients educate their loved ones about their affairs to whatever level of comfort they choose. You don't have to share the specific details or dollar amounts—you can make your points discussing a hypothetical sum—but the more insulated they are from the realities of how you're managing your money, the more vulnerable they will be.

Once you've put your plan together as I suggested—rightsizing your budget, looking for holes, allocating your assets in the way that is best for your future—not only will you know exactly where you stand and what you have, but also it will be possible, and much easier, to pass that knowledge on.

Maybe you can sit in the control tower by yourself. But if you can't, or you won't, then you need to find someone to help you. Many people avoid going to a planner because they are afraid it will be costly. Fortunately for them, they won't be around to see what the lack of planning will cost their heirs.

A good friend with whom I have a social relationship invited me to his house recently. For a very long time, he has run his own affairs, and he's done so very successfully. He's probably one of the brightest investors I have ever met. Since he's well past retirement age, he's recently been giving a lot of thought to the fact that eventually his wife might have the responsibility for managing a very substantial nest egg. But she isn't interested in taking on the job.

I was flattered that he asked me to take over his affairs when the necessity arose. He ushered me into his study and waved in the direction of a wall of green file cabinets. "It's all here," he said. "Everything you need to know is in this room." He thought he was giving me an honor, so he was surprised by my response.

I told him all those files would be a colossal problem. When the day came to take control, I—or my representative—would need days, and more likely weeks, to go through them. The fee for this forensic accounting would be enormous, and the job would be incredibly frustrating. The man had scrupulously held onto everything. Digging through all of the paperwork would be like sequencing his financial DNA.

I told him I was indeed honored, and I hoped he'd be around for many years. "But if you don't sit down and give me a brain dump and a road map—let me know just exactly what's what—I won't feel comfortable doing it," I said.

I'd gone through a similar situation years before. My client was a widow, and her husband also had run his financial affairs without making her privy to any of his decisions. When he died she was confused, overwhelmed, and uncertain of where to begin. That's when she came to me.

I discovered he had in fact done some estate planning (which probably allowed him to convince himself that everything had been taken care of). But he'd done it so long ago that most of the professionals who'd worked on it had passed away. There was no one left to reach out to.

We had to begin the equivalent of an archeological dig. Eventually, to close any gaps, we resorted to having my client bring in every single piece of business-related mail for a full year.

We followed up on all kinds of clues. For example, when the cover note from a credit card solicitation noted that the offer was being made only to "loyal customers," we found a thread to pull. Correctly assuming that he had an account at the bank that had written to him, we managed to recover a couple of thousand dollars. But imagine the wife's ongoing anxiety and frustration in dealing with this task. She was never totally confident that she had found all the missing pieces.

Another unfortunate situation involved a new client who had inherited a sizeable estate from his father. An astute investor, the father had a long-term relationship with a broker. The broker brought him ideas, but what my client hadn't realized was that the dad vetted them and made all the final decisions himself. When he died, the son continued what he mistakenly assumed was his father's lead, giving carte blanche to the broker and ratifying every one of his suggestions.

By the time the son realized that the father had been calling the shots, the estate had already suffered significant losses. At that point, he recognized that he had to educate himself fast or find another advisor. The lesson? If you're leaving someone alone at the wheel, it's imperative to leave a road map.

Many people assume that the documents drafted by an estate lawyer *are* the road map. That's a real misconception. Creating the paperwork isn't the same as estate planning. Some lawyers and accountants may deal only with Who gets it? and How much can we keep from the government? If you want to leave peace and harmony, there are a host of other issues to cover—everything from making sure you've appointed the right fiduciaries to creating a letter that accompanies your will to explain your legacy decisions in complete and nuanced ways that a will cannot do.

I spend a lot of time counseling people on how to plan for their long-term needs and how to pass on their nest egg as efficiently as possible. The real joy for me is making them feel so confident that they will be able to meet all their obligations that they can start thinking about their grander objectives. Asking them to imagine the future and to consider what they want to leave behind is one of the most gratifying tasks I have.

I feel strongly about leaving some kind of mark to show the world that you were here and to pass along your values as well. If you concentrate your entire legacy thinking specifically on the money you leave behind, you're missing a huge opportunity. Money is a tool that you can use to shape people's lives in all kinds of positive ways.

Take the time to sit down and consider how you'd like to impact the world your children and grandchildren will be living in; how you can use your assets to reach those goals; how you can let your descendants know your values, your dreams, and what was important to you. Do you want to fund a house of worship, support medical research and health care, make the environment safer, educate future generations?

Not long ago, only the likes of the Rockefellers, Carnegies, or Mellons could have dreamed of making a difference in the lives of people who were born long after they were gone. Today, you don't have to be in their league to have many options for giving. You can start a family foundation, leave assets to an art museum, or dedicate a chair at a university. Donor-advised funds, with their gamut of choices, provide many ways to position even modest sums so future generations can know what was important to you.

By reclaiming your nest egg, by putting in the effort to do it now and do it correctly, you will know that you've taken control of your financial future and you will have peace of mind. More than that, you will have made it possible to pass your values on to future generations—to turn your success into long-term significance.

Acknowledgments

WHEN I BEGAN WORK on this book it quickly became apparent that it was a collaborative project, and thus many thanks are due.

First, thanks are owed to the countless people over the past 30 years who have entrusted their financial futures to me. My clients, as always, challenge and motivate me to learn more and think harder.

This book would not be nearly as easy for you to read—nor as enjoyable for me to write—without the serendipitous intervention of a person I never met, a writer named Brad Burg. When I realized I needed some assistance getting the knowledge in my head onto paper, I reached out for help. My appeal found its way into Brad's inbox and he put me in touch with his sister, Dale Burg, shortly before he passed away. I never had the opportunity to express my gratitude for his introduction to someone who not only filled the bill but also has become a close friend. I wish I could have said this directly to him: "Thank you, Brad!"

It is impossible for an author to have a better collaborator than Dale Burg. Her patience in pulling things out of me so that they're expressed exactly as I want, and her ability to get my words onto the page and in an organized way have never ceased to amaze me. Her clarity of thought kept me from going off in more directions than a malfunctioning GPS. Working with Dale has helped me become a more effective communicator in all facets of my life. I cannot thank her enough for the countless hours she invested in working on this book and her commitment to its quality.

I am indebted to my agent, Ruth Mills, for her willingness to take on a first-time author and for helping shape my outline into a compelling proposal; to my editor Evan Burton at Bloomberg Press, who saw promise in this book, took up the gauntlet on my behalf, and has made me a published author; and to Laura Walsh, Emilie Herman, and all the folks at Wiley for coming onto the project and seeing it through with enthusiasm and diligence.

Thanks are also due to the people with whom I work at Mercadien:

Jared Reilly, my associate, for all his work with the charts and statistics in this book. He is due a very special thanks for his ability to develop presentations that convey exactly what I am trying to communicate. His skills continually amaze me, and thanks to him, a lot of people think I am smart.

Reggie Burroughs, my colleague, for making me consider with such deliberation what this book should cover. If the phrase, "Measure twice, cut once," didn't already exist, Reg would have coined it himself, and I am grateful for his frequent reminders that I should do just that.

Conrad Druker, my colleague, for his insights and for helping me bear in mind that any lack of clarity on the part of an author can generate an unintended conclusion or action on the part of the reader.

Jamie Diaz, my assistant, for keeping things running smoothly on the days that writing this book took up more working bandwidth than I had anticipated.

I also want to express my appreciation to several people who generously shared their expertise:

Carol Einhorn, who gave me pointers about dealing with long-term care insurance.

Jeff Pearlman, who educated me about the ins and outs of property and casualty insurance.

Patricia Herst, who expanded and clarified the legacy issues I raise in this book.

I am enormously grateful as well to Fareed Zakaria for taking time to share his insights and perspective on the growth and interdependences of world economies.

About the Author

Ken Kamen, president of Mercadien Asset Management, offers comprehensive wealth management consulting services to ultra-affluent individuals, families, and business owners. He specializes in helping his clients work actively with him in developing plans and strategies that are appropriate for their individual situations.

Ken has 30 years of experience in the financial service industries, which he joined while still attending Hofstra University. At 28, he founded Princeton Securities, which he sold in 2000. A former chairman of the National Investment Banking Association, Ken also served as the chairman of a business advisory group that reported to the U.S. House of Representatives' Oversight and Investigations Sub-Committee on financial matters surrounding the Enron corporate scandals.

For his expertise on how Wall Street and Main Street intersect and other financial matters, Ken is frequently quoted in the national media, such as the *Wall Street Journal, USA Today, Forbes, Fortune*, and *BusinessWeek*, and is often invited to appear on CNBC, NBC, ABC, Fox, PBS, and other national and local broadcasts.

Index

Accountants, 187
Accutrade for Windows, 88
Acquisition, assets, 27, 32–33
Active management, 136–137
Adult children, 15–16
Advertising, 60
Advice, unbiased, 188–190
Affirmation, 49–50, 70–71
Aging:
  and asset allocation, 96
  and finances, 15
Amazon.com, 52
American Council of Life
    Insurers, 165
AmeriTrade, 88
Anxiety, 51–52
Appreciation, capital, 151, 157
Asset allocation, 96–99, 102,
    107, 118, 119–120,
    128–130
  aggressive, 156–161
  balanced portfolio, 150–155
  conservative, 144–149
Asset managers, 187
Assets:
  acquisition of, 27, 32–33
  classes of, 128, 135–136
  preservation of, 183–184

retirement (*See* Retirement assets)
retirement needs, 22–23
taxable, 178–179
work as asset class, 37–38

Balance, 117–119
Bank failures, 6
Bear market, 125–126
Behavioral economics, 46, 49, 70
Benchmarking, 31, 50–51
Better-whosis.com, 69
Bezos, Jeff, 51–52
Bias, 70, 75
Bonds, 96
  corporate, 105
  and predictability, 173
  and risk, 104
  as source of income, 103–105
  tax-free, 131
Boomerang phenomenon, 16
BRIC countries, 108
Brokers, 80, 86, 87
Bubble-and-burst lifestyle, 33
Bucket funds, 36
Budgeting, 30–31, 36
Buffett, Warren, 76, 83, 120
Bull market, 124–126
Buying power, 55

Capital appreciation,
    151, 157
Capital gains taxes, 130–131,
    140, 179
Capitalization, 106–107
Capital preservation, 145
Cash, 102–103
    reserves, 119–120
Casualty insurance, 168
CDOs (collateralized debt
    obligations), 83–84
Center for Retirement
    Research, 14
Change, 65
Choice, 49
Coca-Cola, 138
Collateralized debt obligations
    (CDOs), 83–84
Collectibles, 132
Collegegrad.com, 15
Commerce, digital, 109–110
Commissions, 82, 89
Commitment, 56
Commodities, 96, 107–108
Competition, 83
Computers, 136
Confirming bias, 70
Conflicts of interest, 82
Consumer risk, 11
Context, 72
Contrarians, 53–54
Conviction, loss of, 96
Core competencies, 37
Core principles, 115–134
Corporate bonds, 105

Cost basis, 178–179
Credit, structured, 83
Credit cards, 36, 38
Credit defaults, 63
Currency, 96, 102–103
Cutler, Neal, 15

Day trading, 73, 141
Debt, 32, 96
    ongoing, 38–39
Decision making, 46, 66
Decumulation, 169–180
Developed markets, 108
Developing countries, 91
Digital commerce, 109–110
Dilution, 140
Disability insurance, 165
Discipline, 186
Discretionary income, 38
Diversification, 52, 88, 96,
    126–129, 140, 179
Dividends, 106, 140
Donor-advised funds, 201
Dorfman, Dan, 73–74
Dot-com bubble, 6, 106
Dow Jones Industrial Average
    (DJIA), 99–102
Duplication, 126–130

Economics, 46
Efficient Portfolio, 118–119
Electronic media, 66–68
Emerging markets, 108–109
Emotions, 42, 48–49, 129
Equities, 96, 106, 172

E-trading. *See* Online trading
Exchange-traded funds (ETFs), 141

Fear, 128
Federal agency bonds, 105
Fees, 82
Fiduciary responsibility, 87
Financial advisors, 34, 185
Financial crisis of 2008, 6–7, 25,
    81, 86, 92
Financial management,
    personal, 11
Financial planning, 116–117,
    187–190
Financial policy statement, 24
Fitch, 104
401(k)s, 178–179
Framing, 56
Free market, 7

Gain, maximizing, 118–119
Goals, 28–29
    planning for, 116–117
    using as investment guidance,
        56–57
Graham, Benjamin, 120
Gratification, instant, 49
Greenspan, Alan, 7, 84
Gross domestic product
    (GDP), 108
Growth stocks, 105–107, 137–139
Gut, thinking with, 47–48

Head trash, 46–56
Health care, 13–15

Health insurance, 14–15, 35,
    164–165
Healthreform.gov, 164
Hedge funds, 52, 132–133
High yield bonds, 104
Hodges, Jane, 26
Home values, 25–26
Housing bubble, 6, 25–26, 84–85
Hunter mentality, 26–27

Illiquid investments, 132–133
Impulsivity, 47–49, 89
Income:
    and asset allocation, 96
    from bonds, 103–105
    current, 151
    discretionary, 38
    long-term stream, 119–120
    from securities, 140
    working during retirement, 38
Index funds, 139–140
Indexing, 135–136
Individual insecurity, 10
Inflation, 103, 105, 111
Inflation risk, 11
Infomine.ucr.edu, 69
Information, 59
    authenticating, 66–68
    unbiased, 68–74, 75
Inheritance taxes, 168
Instant gratification, 49
Insurance, 163–169, 187. *See also*
    specific insurance, i.e., Health
    insurance
Interest, 140

Interest rates, 104–105, 107
International investments,
    108–110
Internet Corporation for Assigned
    Names and Numbers
    (ICANN), 69
Investment Adviser Act of
    1940, 87
Investments:
  active, 136–137
  conservative, 104, 173
  contrarian, 53–54
  costs, 82
  to create wealth, 41–42
  do-it-yourself, 88
  illiquid, 132–133
  independent research
    agencies, 75
  international, 76, 108–110
  liquid, short-term, 120
  long-term consequences of,
    81–82
  most common mistakes,
    7–8
  objectives, 96
  parable about, 120
  passive, 83, 136–137,
    138–140
  return on, 91
  risk, 11, 44–45
  shopping for, 79
  tricks of the trade, 91–92
  using computers, 136
  volatility, 44–45
IRAs, 178–179

Johnson & Johnson, 138
Judgment, 46
Junk bonds, 104, 186
Justification, 54–55

Laise, Eleanor, 11
Laissez-faire, 7
Large cap companies, 112, 136
Lawyers, 187
Layaway plans, 38
Liability insurance, 168
Librarians' Index (lii.com), 69
Life expectancy, 11–12
Life insurance, 167–168, 184
Life policy statement, 24
Lifestyle, retirement, 3
  sustainability of, 174–178
Longevity risk, 3, 11–12, 174
Long-term bonds, 105
Long-term care insurance,
    165–167
Loss aversion, 44–45, 56

Madoff, Bernie, 52, 63
Managed funds, 140
Margin buying, 131
Market capitalization, 106
Market segments, 139–143
Market timing, 49, 97, 124–126
Markowitz, Harry M., 97, 118
Mark to market, 104
May Day, 82–83
Media, 59, 63–64. *See also* News
    coverage
    electronic, 66–68

Medical insurance. *See* Health
    insurance
Medicare, 14, 35, 164
Medigap, 164
Mid-cap companies, 136
Millennials, 16
Millionaires, 45
Minimum fixed commission rates,
    82–83
Modern portfolio theory, 97
Money:
    attitude about, 41
    management, 184–185,
        187–190
    personal relationship to, 45
Moody's, 104
Morningstar, 75
Mortgage-backed securities, 105
Mortgages, 6–7, 25, 38, 84–85
    subprime, 76
Mountain chart, 111
Mr. Market, 120–121
Municipal bonds, 105
Mutual funds, 139–140, 142
    international, 76

Net asset value (NAV), 140
NetworkSolutions.com, 69
News coverage, 64–65, 71–72.
    See also Media
Noise, 59–77
    filtering, 68–74

Online information, 66–68
Online trading, 88–90

Opinion networks, 71
Opportunity, 53
Outliving resources, 18

Par, 103
Paralysis by analysis, 186
Paranoia, 47
Passive investments, 83, 136–137,
    139–140
Patterns, 98
Pensions, 9, 10
Percentages, philosophy of,
    129–130
Perception, 48, 106, 139
Performance, 28–29
Personalizing, 49–51
Perspective, 55–56
Phantom diversification,
    126–127, 142
Philosophy of percentages,
    129–130
Phoenix Affluent Marketing
    Service, 45
Polling, 71
Ponzi schemes, 52, 63, 91
Portfolio:
    aggressive allocation, 156–161
    balanced allocation, 150–155
    conservative, 144–149
    diversification (*See* Diversification)
    reconstructing, 135–162
    samples of, 143–161
Portfolio theory, 97
Predictability, 173
Price discovery, 136

Priorities, retirement, 23–24
Property insurance, 168
Prospectus, 82, 86
Psychology, 46
Public relations, 60–62
Purchasing power, 111

Quality of life, 14
Quants, 83

Rate of return, 96
Ratings agencies, bonds, 104
Rationalization, 54–55, 92
Read, Daniel, 49
Real estate, 96, 107, 132
Real estate investment trusts
    (REITs), 107
Reason, 51–52
Registered representatives, 80
Relative value, 136–137
Replacement income, 165
Resources, outliving, 18
Retirement:
    concerns about planning, 18
    priorities, 23–24
    realistic expectations about,
        34–35
    redefining, 8–9
Retirement assets:
    and lifestyle sustainability,
        176–177
    order of withdrawal from,
        178–180
    what is needed, 22–23
    withdrawing from, 171–174

Retirement planning:
    goals *versus* returns, 28–29
Retirement safety zone,
    176–177
Returns, 28–29
Risk, 11
    anticipating, 18
    and asset allocation, 96
    and bonds, 104
    coming to terms with, 24–26
    high-stakes, 27–28
    investment, 44–45, 81
    minimizing, 118–119
    offloading, 163–164
    tolerance, 42–43
    and volatility, 121–124
Roth accounts, 179–180
Russell 2000, 136, 137
Ryan, Tim, 76

Samuelson, Paul, 74
Sandwich generation, 15–17
Sarbanes-Oxley Act, 6
Savings:
    to create wealth, 41–42
Scandals, corporate, 6
Securities:
    income from, 140
Securities and Exchange
    Commission (SEC), 87
Securities Exchange Act, 87
Securities Industry and Financial
    Markets Association
    (SIFMA), 76
Security, 27

Self-interest, 7
Self-reliance, 34
Sense of urgency, 64, 91
Separately managed accounts
    (SMAs), 141–142
Shorr, Daniel, 59
Short stocks, 68
Skills, transferable, 37
Small cap companies, 81, 112,
    136
SMAs (separately managed
    accounts), 141–142
Smith, Adam, 7
Social media, 66–68
Social Security, 9–10
Society of Actuaries, 116
S&P 500, 99, 122–124,
    125–126, 136
Spending, tracking, 36
S&P MidCap 400, 136
Standard & Poor's, 75, 104
Stocks, 96
    commissions, 82–83
    diversification, 88
    for growth, 105–107,
        137–139
    power of, 110–112
    shorting, 68
    value stocks, 137–139
Style quilt, 97–99
Subprime mortgages, 76
Supply and demand, 108
Survival responses, 47
Sustainable rate of withdrawal,
    171–174

Tax-deferred accounts, 179
Taxes:
    and asset allocation, 96
    capital gains, 130–131, 140,
        179
    inheritance, 168
    and mutual funds, 140–141
    and retirement asset
        withdrawals, 178–179
Tax-free bonds, 131
Tax-free investments,
    179–180
Technology, 66
Television, 65
Term, bond, 104–105
Threads, 67
Threats, response to, 48
Time horizon, 96, 124
Trade-up generation, 32–33
Tranches, 83
Treasury bills, 105, 111–112
Trends, 74
Trustworthiness, 74–75
Tylenol, 138

Umbrella liability insurance,
    168–169
Uncertainty, 45–46
Urgency, sense of, 64, 91

Value, relative, 136–137
ValueLine, 75
Value stocks, 137–139
Value trap, 139
Van Leeuwen, Barbara, 49

Volatility, 44–45, 48, 72–74, 96,
    112, 117–119, 169
  and risk, 121–124
von Bismarck, Otto, 8
Vulnerability, 95

Wealth, 29
  creation, 41–42
  insurance, 163
Webb, Anthony, 15
Web optimization, 68
Web sites:
  credibility of, 69–70
  proprietary, 70

Well-being, 27
Withdrawal rate:
  and lifestyle sustainability,
    176–177
  order, 178–180
  from retirement assets,
    171–174
Work:
  during retirement,
    37–38

Zakaria, Fareed, 110
Zhivan, Natalia, 15